Happy as a Lark

A Handbook of Happiness

SREETI AMONKAR

NOTION PRESS

Dedication

Namo Tassa Bhagavato Arahato Sammā Sambudhassa

Homage to the blessed One, the Perfected One, the Fully Awakened One

***

Namo Tassa Bhagavato Arahato Sammā Sambudhassa

Homage to the blessed One, the Perfected One, the Fully Awakened One

***

Namo Tassa Bhagavato Arahato Sammā Sambudhassa

Homage to the blessed One, the Perfected One, the Fully Awakened One

***

Dedicated to the Sonawane Family- Prakash Dada, Krushna Tai, Priyanka, and Prashant, for making me a part of their family and giving me a home away from home.

And to my fur-baby- Butsu, for forcing me to take a break and chill when I got too immersed in my work and thus, taking care of my emotional and physical fitness

Table of Contents

Foreword.. i

Preface..iii

Aknowledgements..ix

Introduction...xii

1. Why we are Unhappy___________________________1

2. Creating Happines___________________________11

3. Making Space_______________________________23

4. A Way of Life_______________________________44

5. An inward Journey___________________________55

6. Happy mind in a healthy body______________80

7. We are what we eat__________________________95

8. Break free_________________________________106

Foreword

Sreeti has always been a wonderful communicator. She has always maintained a log of what she does, practiced extensive journaling and has also posted extensively. This gives people she knows a wonderful sense of what she is doing.

When I went through the book and mapped it against what I know Sreeti to have been doing, I found a remarkable congruence between what she has been doing and what she has written in the book. Which highlights brilliantly the fact that she walks the talk. This says a lot about the quality of the writing because Sreeti is an accomplished practitioner of spiritual practices and has courageously confronted many difficult situations in her life.

The book provides immense hope for the readers, reassuring them that happiness is not something that can be attained only after having achieved significant landmarks in terms money power and status. The heartening news that the book provides is that all the resources we have for happiness are within us.

The book takes us on a journey of all the methods that we can use to make life easier for ourselves. While it is packed with powerful learning insights, it also offers eminently doable practical exercises and there are many parts of it that one can use as a workbook as well.

A wonderful feature is that it is not prescriptive in nature. It allows the reader to pick and choose what they would like to retain and practice, and what they would like to discard, if at all. It has a universal appeal, meaning it is equally useful for every belief system. The approach is one of amazing empathy, recognizing that different people have different temperaments and therefore may like to use different methodologies.

Being practical and also highly action oriented, it nudges people out of their comfort zone, encouraging them to be proactive and take risks for a noble pursuit.

By nature of its versatility, it is highly recommended reading across age groups and professions. You will love your decision

Milind Kher

**Emotional Intelligence Specialist,
NLP Practitioner,
ICF certified life coach**
01-July-2020

Preface

-Dalai Lama XIV

What makes the world go round? In my opinion, it is happiness. You might disagree and say that it's money. However, the very reason why people try to amass money is that they think that it will buy security, power, luxury, pleasure, comfort, and other things which they desire. In today's world, money and the things money can buy, tangible like all material possessions and intangible like financial security, power, fame, etc. have turned out to be our substitute for happiness. This is due to our ignorance of what real happiness is.

Time and again it has been proved that money can't buy us happiness. It can only buy things that give us pleasure. This feeling of pleasure which is mistaken for happiness is very shallow and transitory. A misconception that happiness and pleasure are one and the same, and that it can be purchased like a commodity, is common and widespread. Fortuitously at the same time, more and more people have begun to realize that happiness is something altogether different. These evolved people have set out on a journey that has led them in an inwards direction.

I too embarked on a similar journey a couple of decades ago. The necessity of this pursuit of happiness arose out of a profound sense of unhappiness and extreme levels of stress while growing up. As a child, I was abandoned by my mother and neglected by my father. I was raised by relatives who outrightly hated me and thought of me as a burden. My childhood and teenage years can be described as an ocean of misery in which I kept swimming in the hope of someday finding some land to rest on.

As I grew up, I turned into a volatile person. Angry, confused, and extremely sad. I started struggling to find a way out of the loveless home in which I lived. This so-called home was more like a prison to me. In my teenage years and early adulthood, I started struggling harder to find an escape from my miserable life. I was parched for happiness and peace and had no clue where to find it.

My quest for happiness forced me to go pillar to post. From joining a far-leftist student organization, which was needless to say, atheist, to visiting several ashrams, following spiritual gurus, and practicing various paths and cults. Of course, all of these endeavors helped me in one way or the other.

It was not a surprise that my self-esteem was lower than my ankles and I chose to marry a bum and ended up not just emotionally but physically abused and battered. This drove me into a deep pit of clinical depression. Luckily with the help of a neighbor and her family I was able to recover. On the advice of my father (the only good advice I ever got from him) I attended a ten-day vipassana retreat conducted by SN Goenka. That was a turning point in my life. I started accepting my misfortune with grace. I learned to look at life with equanimity. It was easier said than done.

I moved to pune soon after that. found myself a job and tried to live a normal life. With my hard work, I became a voice and accent trainer. The year was 2000 and Pune was experiencing an IT-boom. In it, I must say, I got lucky.

Though I was doing well in my career, my miserable past kept haunting me. I keept getting panic attacks and nightmares keept me awake all night. One thing I was sure of was that I did not want to start taking drugs for my mental agony again because though they gave me some relief, I used to become emotionally numb, or like a zombie, when I took them.

So I decided to try alternate healing therapies. I learnt Neuro Linguistic Programming, Transactional Analysis, Emotional Freedom Technique, Hypnotism, Expressive Arts Therapy, Psychodrama, Pranic Healing, and Art of Living. I also took life coaching. All these courses and the learnings I got from them not only helped me in healing my traumas but also, I became very good at helping others. I also became a successful behavioral trainer and a life coach who is well known to help my clients reclaim their happiness.

All these adventures and explorations made a drastic paradigm shift in the way I perceived happiness. At least, I understood what happiness was not. I met so many people with varied natures. And from this I inferred that happiness is contagious and that with our attitude and behavior we can make ourselves and others either happy or miserable. This insight that I got from all my years of chasing happiness has made me believe, in sharing my happiness with whoever comes in contact with me on the journey of my life. And also share my experiences and what worked for me. It may or may not work for you completely. But even if a few things from this book help some of you to feel a little bit better, I will feel grateful and fulfilled.

In the meanwhile, you can try doing some of the things which I have practiced and wish to share with you. These are techniques taught by masters over the centuries. I am only a humble practitioner and compiler.

Sreeti Amonkar

01-May-20

Acknowledgments

I would like to acknowledge all the people who have helped directly or indirectly in writing this book. However, some contributors deserve a special mention.

A special thanks to my mentor, Mr Arfeen Khan, under whose guidance I have written this book in such a short period.

It would have been impossible without the consistent guidance and insights from Mr. Prashant Sonawane, who is no less than a family to me. He is a Corporate Trainer, and an Independent Researcher in Buddhist Philosophy. I especially loved the title he came up with for this book.

Mr. Milind Kher Is a well-known and highly respected person in the training community and has been a go to person to several trainers and coaches including me. I am thankful to him for graciously accepting to write a foreword for this book.

I hope that this book satisfies the purpose for which you have picked it up. I wish you happy reading and most of all a happy life.

Introduction

Our search of happiness in life is very much like that of the male musk deer. The deer keeps wandering in the forest in search of the source a sweet fragrance which is so enchanting. He wonders 'where is this enchanting smell is coming from?' Paradoxically he is oblivious to the fact that the alluring scent is exuded by his own body. From a gland in his own navel. He spends his whole life in ignorance chasing this aroma in vain.

Don't we humans have a similar illusion about happiness? Why are we searching for it everywhere else in the world, when we can find it within, within our innate self? When are we going to shift our paradigm about happiness and set ourselves free from the shackles of misconceptions?

Finding answers to such questions will need patience. Finding your real self and your purpose of existence will need persistence. Finding happiness in its real form will need determination. Together, with patience, persistence, and perseverance, you will start experiencing pure bliss. You will be free from all negativity and become one with true happiness. And this pursuit of happiness will bring peace from within which will shine upon your world.

Imagine a world where every single human understands the fact that happiness is not something extrinsic. It is to be felt within and not without. By within, I mean inside yourself and in every moment. It may be momentary or may last for a lifetime, but it remains inside you. Happiness is immaterial of worldly things. You need not be a millionaire to be happy; you just need to feel it without greed, without arrogance, without ignorance. Once this thought takes form, the world will be free of hatred and will overflow with love. When love takes over, it brings an abundance of happiness.

With the advance of modern technology, life has become easier, people have more money and comforts. Why then the majority of us are unhappy in some way or the other? I think one of the reasons for our unhappiness could be that we have become too greedy and materialistic. We are more focused on gathering more and more. Whether it is fame and fortune or power and prestige. Unfortunately, the desire for this is never-ending. It is an endless pit.

Prosperity and automation have made our lives more comfortable and easier. But has it made us any happier? I think not. One of the reasons for this could be because we have unconsciously developed certain habits which act as the breeding grounds of unhappiness.

Happiness looks different to different people. For you, maybe it's being at peace with who you are. Or having a secure network of friends who accept you unconditionally. Or the freedom to pursue your deepest dreams. Whatever your version of true happiness is, you can always reach for it or at least walk towards it.

Chapter 1

***

Why Are We Unhappy?

With the advance of modern technology, life has become easier, people have more money and comforts. Why then the majority of us are unhappy in some way or the other? I think the reason for our unhappiness is that we have become too materialistic. We are more focused on gathering material things. Unfortunately, the desire for this is never-ending. It is an endless pit.

The modern-day progress has made our lives easier and comfortable but not any happier. That's because we are not enhancing our level of consciousness which would lead to the understanding of the things which matter.

Some of the reasons for our unhappiness could be:

Comparison with Others

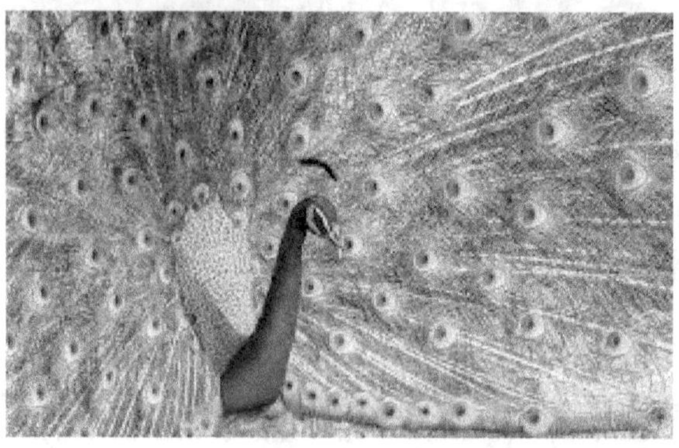

There is this story about a peacock and a crow.

Once, there was a crow who lived in a forest and was satisfied in life. But one day he saw a beautiful swan and thought to himself, "This swan is so white and beautiful, and

I am so black and hence unpleasant to the eye. This swan must be the happiest bird in the world."

He expressed his thoughts to the swan. "Actually," the swan replied, "I was feeling that I was the happiest bird around until I saw a parrot, which has two colours. I now think the parrot is the happiest bird in creation." The crow then approached the parrot. The parrot explained, "I lived a very happy life until I saw a peacock. I have only two colours, but the peacock has multiple colours."

The crow then visited a peacock in the zoo and saw that hundreds of people had gathered to see him. After the people had left, the crow approached the peacock. "Dear peacock," the crow said, "you are so beautiful. Every day thousands of people come to see you. When people see me, they immediately shoo me away. I think you are the happiest bird on the planet."

The peacock replied, "I always thought that I was the most beautiful and happy bird on the planet. But because of my beauty, I am entrapped in this zoo. I have examined the zoo very carefully, and I have realized that the crow is the only bird not kept in a cage. So, for the past few days, I have been thinking that if I were a crow, I could happily roam everywhere."

Comparison with ourselves brings improvement, comparison with others bring discontent.

Comparing ourselves with others will make us unhappy. We might inadvertently be comparing the strength of another person with our weaknesses, which would be unfair to ourselves. If you focus on your strengths, you will multiply them. However, if we focus on our weakness, at the best we will become mediocre and at the worst, frustrated.

Each one of us has a different journey to success. We have circumstances, obstacles, and opportunities. Each one of us has our unique abilities.

The right approach is to get inspired by others and not compare with them.

Real happiness comes from satisfaction. If we have given our best to whatever we are doing, we will have a sense of satisfaction, which is the real source of happiness.

The sense of 'I'm not enough" "I'm not rich enough", "beautiful enough"," smart enough" etc. creates sadness within ourselves. Keep saying to yourself "I'm enough".

You are stuck in your comfort zone

A comfort zone is a beautiful place, but nothing grows there.

The following poem by an anonymous poet sums up the story of the life of a person stuck in a comfort zone until he thought of venturing out.

I used to have a comfort zone where I knew I wouldn't fail.
The same four walls and busywork were really more like jail.
I longed so much to do the things I'd never done before,
But stayed inside my comfort zone and paced the same old floor.

I said it didn't matter that I wasn't doing much.
I said I didn't care for things like commission checks and such.
I claimed to be so busy with the things inside my zone,
But deep inside I longed for something special of my own.

I couldn't let my life go by just watching others win.
I held my breath; I stepped outside and let the change begin.

I took a step and with new strength, I'd never felt before,
I kissed my comfort zone good-bye and closed and locked the door

If you're in the comfort zone, afraid to venture out,
Remember that all winners were at one time filled with
doubt.
A step or two and words of praise can make your dreams
came true

Reach   for   your   future   with   a   smile;
Success is there for you!

One of the most common reasons for the lack of happiness in people's lives is a lack of growth. At some point in time in our lives, we get stuck in our comfort zone. Most of us try to play safe all the time and call this 'being practical'.

We don't pull up our courage to do what we want to do or what we must do to progress. We don't put efforts to realise our dreams, or worse still, we don't dare to dream at all.

All our lives we live a mediocre life and regret when it is too late. Most common remorse of people on their death bed is that they wished they dared to live a life true to themselves and not the life others expected of them.

Sometimes we think that we are too young or too old for trying out something different. At other times we think that our circumstances are not right yet. There are times when we think too much about what if we fail. The lack of courage to come out of our comfort zone makes us unhappy about our lives.

Not being in the present moment

We are either brooding over our past or worrying about our future. This whole focus on past and future makes us unable to enjoy our present moment and that becomes the reason for our unhappiness.

This incident given below will tell us the difference in the attitude of a person annoyed at the past and anxious about the future and someone who lives in the present.

On a busy Monday morning, the young mom shouted out at her husband, "Honey, would you drop the kids off to school today? I've got a lot of chores to complete and errands to run."

Not too happy with the request the husband agreed in a grumbling tone. He yelled at the kids, "Hurry up, kids! I don't have all day."

So, the father and the kids jumped into the car and drove off. The busy father glancing at his watch fumed. "My wife could have easily finished off her chores yesterday when it was a holiday. This last-minute task is going to make me late for work. My boss won't be too happy about it. What if he's already in a bad mood?"

While he was complaining about the past and worrying about the future, his car approached a railway crossing. Just as he reached there, the safety gate closed down right in front of him. As expected, he banged his fist on the dashboard and groaned saying, "Dammit! I'm going to be held up by a train and be delayed further."

As the dad was fuming in the front seat, anxiously tapping his fingers on the steering wheel, reviewing, in his mind, how to make up some time … a sweet little voice of a child, calls out from the backseat: "Daddy, Daddy, we're so lucky! We get to watch the train go by!"

The point to remember is that we can't ever go back and undo the action of the past. Similarly, we cannot go to the future and make things happen now.

The only place where we can be is, in the present. Being in the present is very relaxing. Just as the child in the present was happy and relaxed as against his father who was stressed.

Be in the present with all your senses. Listen to the sounds, observe the colors and shapes of the things around. Feel the texture of the things you touch; taste the food you eat. Be aware of the smells.

"If you are depressed you are living in the past. If you are anxious you are living in the future. If you are at peace you are living in the present."

- Lao Tzu

Tying your happiness to something or someone

Most people think that happiness is possible only on the happening of certain events and not before. You must have heard statements like the ones below from others, and you might have found yourself thinking these thoughts: I'll be happy when I own a luxury car, a big house, or a perfect partner or when I have a big fat bank account. I'll be happy when I have the latest version of the iPhone. Diamonds will make me happy. A certain Job or a certain place will make me happy.

What's common in all the above statements?

In all such cases, we tie our happiness to the happening of some event or certain material possession. This makes our happiness conditional.

Setting a criterion for our happiness is like running after a mirage. Once you reach a certain point, you start to look for something more. And hence happiness keeps eluding us.

Does that mean we should not have goals or dreams? Of course not. On the contrary, it's wonderful to think big and go after big goals. There is nothing wrong with that. The problem is when we tie our happiness with the happening of those events, we put ourselves into a vicious circle because we set conditions for our happiness.

The best way is to get excited about and strive to achieve the goal, but at the same time, be joyful and enjoy the journey.

So, what should we do? I believe that our objective should be to attain the level of happiness which is unconditional.

"I am determined to be cheerful and happy in whatever situation I may find myself. I have learned that the greater part of our misery or unhappiness is determined not by our circumstance but by our disposition."

-Martha Washington

Unconditional happiness is something that should be our ultimate goal because then you can control it on your own. You can be happy right here and now.

You don't need any big material possessions or other people or any other conditions to become happy. You can just become happier in the present moment. Being happy in no manner means not being sincere or serious about your goals; being happy increases your chances of achieving your goals.

Chapter 2

***

Creating Happiness

Establishing rituals is of paramount importance if you want to break the old habit patterns which make you unhappy and imbibe new habits which make you happy. If you've ever tried breaking a bad habit, you know all too well how ingrained it is. Well, good habits are deeply engrained, too. Why not work on making positive habits a part of your routine?

Let's take a look at some daily, monthly, and yearly habits to help kickstart your quest. Just remember that everyone's version of happiness is a little different, and so is their path to achieving it. If some of these habits create added stress or just don't fit into your lifestyle, ditch them. With a little time and practice, you'll figure out what does and doesn't work for you.

Project Happiness

"Smiling is the best way to face every problem, to crush every fear, and to hide every pain."

-Will Smith

Smile. Even if you are not happy, act as if you are. You tend to smile when you're happy however, it's actually a two-way street. We smile because we're happy, and smiling causes the brain to release dopamine, which makes us happier.

That doesn't mean you have to go around with a fake smile plastered on your face all the time. But the next time you find yourself feeling low, crack a smile, and see what happens. Or try starting each morning by smiling at yourself in the mirror.

Smile

We crack a smile—a genuine eye crinkle which is called a "Duchenne smile"—our cardiovascular system calms. Laughing takes it one step further. Partly because it forces us to exhale. Simply exhaling lowers our heart rate and induces feelings of calm.

Smiling releases endorphins, which combat stress hormones. My suggestion is, "You should practice smiling right now, even if you feel foolish. You're cancelling some of the stress cortisol and you're increasing your happiness—a double bonus." So,enjoy the funny side.

Breathe deeply

You're tensed, your shoulders are tight, and you feel as though you just might collapse. We all know that feeling. Instinct may tell you to take a long, deep breath to calm yourself down. Turns out, that instinct is a good one.

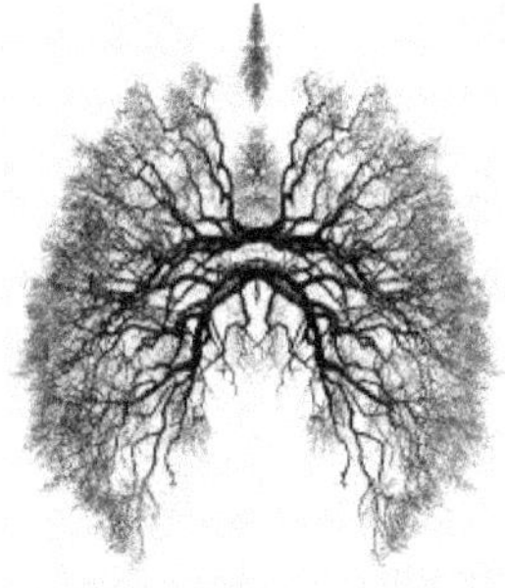

According to Harvard Health, deep breathing exercises can help reduce stress.

The next time you feel stressed or are at your wit's end, work through these steps:

1. Close your eyes. Try to envision a happy memory or a beautiful place.
2. Take a slow, deep breath.
3. Slowly breathe out through your mouth.
4. Repeat this process several times, until you start to feel calm.

If you're having a hard time taking slow, deliberate breaths, try counting to 5 in your head with each inhales and exhales.

Acknowledge the unhappy moments

A positive attitude is generally a good thing, but bad things happen to everyone. It's just part of life. If you get some bad news, make a mistake, or just feel like you are stuck, don't try to pretend you're happy.

Acknowledge the feeling of unhappiness, letting yourself experience it for a moment. Then, shift your focus toward what made you feel this way and what it might take to recover. Would a deep breathing exercise help? A long walk outside? Talking it over with someone? Let the moment pass and take care of yourself. Remember, no one's happy all the time.

Keep a journal

"Journaling is like whispering to one's self and listening at the same time."

-Mina Murray

A journal is a good way to organize your thoughts,

analyse your feelings, and make plans. And you don't have to be a literary genius or write volumes to benefit. It can be as simple as jotting down a few thoughts before you go to bed. If putting certain things in writing makes you nervous, you can always shred it when you've finished. It's the process that counts.

Declutter

"Clutter is the physical manifestation of unmade decisions fuelled by procrastination."

—Christina Scalise

Decluttering sounds like a big project, but setting aside just 20 minutes a week can have a big impact. Decluttering doesn't happen overnight. It's a process—and often, one that requires equal parts motivation and inspiration.

What can you do in 20 minutes? Lots. Here are some tips.

1. Set a timer on your phone and take 15 minutes to tidy up a specific area of one room — say, your closet or that out-of-control junk drawer. Put everything in its place and toss or give away any extra clutter that's not serving you anymore.
2. Keep a designated box for giveaways to make things a little easier (and avoid creating more clutter).
3. Use the remaining 5 minutes to do a quick walk through your living space, putting away whatever stray items end up in your path.

You can do this trick once a week, once a day, or anytime you feel like your space is getting out of control.

See Friends

Socialize- Join some club, connect with your old friends, make new friends. Humans are social beings, and having close friends can make us happier. Who do you miss? Reach out to them. Make a date to get together or simply have a long phone chat. In adulthood, it can feel next to impossible to make new friends. But it's not about how many friends you have. It's about having meaningful relationships — even if it's just with one or two people.

Try getting involved in a local volunteer group or taking a class. Both can help to connect you with like-minded people in your area. And chances are, they're looking for friends, too. Companionship doesn't have to be limited to other humans. Pets can offer similar benefits. Love animals but can't have a pet? Consider volunteering at a local animal shelter to make some new friends — both human and animal.

However, you must choose your friends carefully. You are the average of the five friends you hang out with. Choosing your friends wisely is one of the most important factors related to happiness. Do you have some friends who are energy vampires? Energy vampires are those who drain your energy when you're around them. Perhaps they're frequently complaining and reminding you of negative events? Try to stay away from such toxic people, and mingling with optimistic people, who make you feel positive and energized. Purchasing material items like televisions, clothes, jewellery, and cars won't make you happier. All they do is give momentary happiness. Humans beings are social animals. We derive happiness and satisfaction from social connections. Hence, I suggest that we invest time and money in people who contribute to our growth. Socialise, spend some quality time with family, friends, colleagues. Go for outings, concerts, yoga retreat, a holiday to some exotic destination, etc.

Plan your week

"If you fail to plan, you are planning to fail!"

- Benjamin Franklin

Feel like you're flailing about? Sit down at the end of every week and make a basic list for the following week. Even if you don't stick to the plan, blocking out time where you can do laundry, go grocery shopping, or tackle projects at work can help to quiet your mind.

You can get a fancy planner, but even a sticky note on your computer or piece of scrap paper in your pocket can do the job.

Unplug

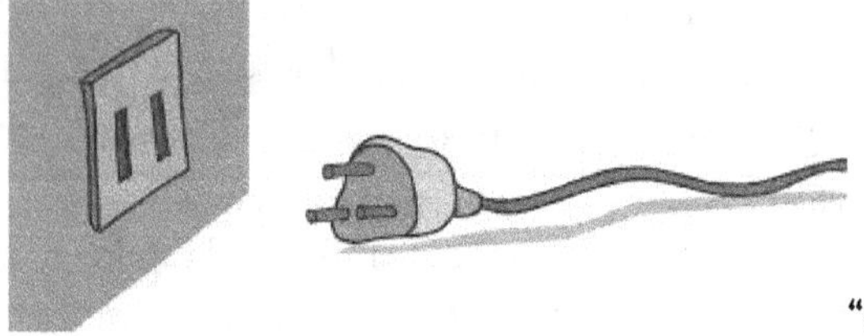

"Being connected to everything has disconnected us from ourselves and the preciousness of this present moment."
— L.M. Browning

Ditch your phone. Turn off all the electronics and put those earbuds away for at least one hour once a week. They'll still be there for you later. If you still want them, that is.

If you haven't unplugged in a while, you might be surprised at the difference it makes. Let your mind wander free for a change. Read. Meditate. Take a walk and pay attention to your surroundings. Be sociable. Or be alone. Just be.

Sounds too daunting? Try doing a shorter amount of time several times a week.

Find a self-care ritual

"Love yourself first, and everything else falls in line. You really have to love yourself to get anything done in this world."

- Lucille Ball

It's easy to neglect self-care in a fast-paced world. However, since your body carries your thoughts, passions, and spirit through this world, doesn't it deserve a little love?

Maybe it's unwinding your workweek with a long, hot bath. Or adopting a skincare routine that makes you feel indulgent. Or simply setting aside a night to put on your softest jammies and watch a movie from start to finish. A relaxing massage once a week can do wonders for your body and mind. Whatever it is, make time for it. Put it in your planner if you must, but do it.

Treat Yourself to a day out

"You have to treat yourself every once in a while, get to the fun stuff!"

-Heidi Klum

No one to go out with? Well, what rule says you can't go out alone? Go to your favourite restaurant, watch a movie, or go on that trip you've always dreamed of. Even if you're a social butterfly, spending some deliberate time alone can help you reconnect with the activities that truly make you happy.

Take time to reflect

"Life can only be understood backward, but it must be lived forward."

-Soren Kierkegaard

The start of a new year is a good time to stop and take inventory of your life. Set aside some time to catch up with yourself the way you would with an old friend and introspect on the following:

1. How are you doing?
2. What have you been up to?
3. Are you happier than you were a year ago?

Please avoid the pitfalls of judging yourself too harshly for your answers. You've made it to another year, and that itself is plenty.

If you find that your mood hasn't improved much over the last year, consider hiring a coach or making an appointment with a counsellor or talking to a therapist. You might be dealing with depression or even an underlying physical condition that's impacting your mood. To rule that out it would be wise to consult a doctor.

Re-evaluate your goals

"You have to keep recycling yourself."

-Chuck Palahniuk

People change, so think about where you're heading and consider if that's still where you want to go. There's no shame in changing your game.

Let go of any goals that no longer serve you, even if they sound nice on paper.

Take care of your body

It's been said that a healthy mind resides in a healthy body. Your physical and mental health are closely intertwined. Regular exercise not only keeps you healthy but also happy.

Making Space

To make space for happiness we need to get rid of some of the rubbish we have collected in our life. The following are some of the ways to cleanse your heart and refurbish it.

Forgiveness

When another person hurts us, it can overturn our lives. Sometimes the hurt is very deep, especially when a spouse or a parent betrays our trust, or when we are victims of a crime, or when we've been harshly bullied. Anyone who has suffered a grievous hurt knows that when our inner world is badly disrupted, it's difficult to concentrate on anything other than our turmoil or pain. When we hold on to hurt, we are emotionally crippled, and our relationships suffer. This leads to profound unhappiness. We have two choices, one to self- sabotage with self-pity and suffering or forgive and let go. Forgiveness is the only remedy for this. When life hits us hard, there is nothing as effective as forgiveness for healing deep wounds. I am saying this from my own experience.

Agreed, the suffering may have had a deep impact on your life, your peace of mind, however, 'letting go' of these feelings will help you move on with life with a renewed vigor and hope.

Forgiveness is about goodness, about extending mercy to those who've harmed us, even if they don't deserve it. It is not about finding excuses for the offending person's behavior or pretending it didn't happen. Nor is there a quick formula you can follow. Forgiveness is a process that involves efforts. However, it's worth it. Working on forgiveness can help us increase our self-esteem and give us a sense of inner strength and safety. It can reverse the lies that we often tell ourselves when someone has hurt us deeply—lies like, "I am defeated" or "I'm not worthy." Forgiveness can heal us and allow us to move on in life with meaning and purpose. Forgiveness matters, and we will be its primary beneficiary.

It's important to figure out who has hurt you and how. This may seem obvious, but not every action that causes you suffering is unjust. For example, you don't need to forgive your child or your spouse for being imperfect, even if their imperfections are inconvenient for you.

Forgiveness is always hard when we are dealing with deep injustices from others. I have known people who refuse to use the word forgiveness because it just makes them so angry. That's OK—we all have our timelines for when we can be merciful. But if you want to forgive and are finding it hard you can try Metta meditation.

First remember that if you are struggling with forgiveness, that doesn't mean you're a failure at forgiveness. Forgiveness is a process that takes time, patience, and determination. Try not to be harsh on yourself, but be gentle and foster a sense of quiet within, an inner acceptance of yourself. Try to respond to yourself as you would to someone whom you love deeply.

Surround yourself with good and wise people who support you and who have the patience to allow you time to heal in your way. Also, practice humility—not in the sense of putting yourself down, but in realizing that we are all capable of imperfection and suffering.

Try to develop courage and patience in yourself to help you in the journey. Also, if you practice bearing small slights against you without lashing out, you give a gift to everyone—not only to the other person but to everyone whom that person may harm in the future because of your anger. You can help end the cycle of inflicting pain on others.

If you are still finding it hard to forgive, you can choose to practice with someone easier to forgive—maybe someone who hurt you in a small way, rather than deeply. Alternatively, it can be better to focus on forgiving the person who is at the root of your pain—may be an abusive parent or a spouse who betrayed you. If these hurts impact other parts of your life and other relationships, it may be necessary to start there.

Forgive yourself. Most of us tend to be harder on ourselves than we are on others and we struggle to love ourselves. If you are not feeling lovable because of some things you have done, you may need to work on self-forgiveness and offer to yourself what you offer to others who have hurt you: a sense of inherent worth, despite your actions.

In self-forgiveness, you honor yourself as a person, even if you are imperfect. If you've seriously broken your standards, there is a danger of sliding into self-loathing. When this happens, you may not take good care of yourself—you might overeat or oversleep or start smoking or engage in other forms of "self-punishment." You need to recognize this and move toward self-compassion. Soften your heart toward yourself.

After you have been able to self-forgive, you will also need to engage in seeking forgiveness from others whom you've harmed and right the wrongs as best as you can. It's important to be prepared for the possibility that the other person may not be ready to forgive you and to practice patience and humility. But, a sincere apology, free of conditions and expectations, will go a long way toward your receiving forgiveness in the end.

Metta Meditation

Develop Metta (Loving Kindness)

Metta is the practice of cultivating universal love, friendliness, or lovingkindness. Metta is benevolence toward all beings, without discrimination or selfish attachment. Metta can be compared to the unconditional love that a mother would have for her children. This love does not discriminate between benevolent people and malicious people. It is a love in which "I" and "you" disappear, and where there is no possessor and nothing to

possess. By practicing Metta, one can overcome anger, ill will, hatred, and aversion. It is an excellent meditation for forgiveness and letting go of grudges.

The practice progresses in five stages. As we use Metta during meditation, we cultivate Metta for:

1. Ourselves
2. A good friend
3. A neutral person — someone we don't have any strong feelings for
4. A difficult person — someone we have conflicts with or feelings of ill will towards
5. All sentient beings

In your practice, you can access Metta through meditation and identifying someone at each of the stages. Learning to accept all for how they are will give you the freedom to love and forgive.

Metta Meditation Script

1. Find a comfortable position in which to sit for this period. As you allow your eyes to gently close, tune into the body, and make any minor adjustments. It can be helpful to remember our intentions of both ease and awareness. Sit in a way that feels comfortable but alert.

2. We'll start with a few minutes of concentration practice, just to help our minds settle and arrive in our present time experience.

3. As you allow the body to resume natural breathing, see where in the body you can feel the breath. It may be in

the stomach or abdomen, where you can feel the rising and falling as we breathe. It might be in the chest, where you may notice the expansion and contraction as the body inhales and exhales. Perhaps it's at the nostrils, where you can feel a slight tickle as the air comes in, and the subtle warmth as the body exhales. You can pick one spot to stick with for this meditation practice.

4. As you feel the body breathing, try to stay with the breath all the way through. Stick with it from the beginning of the inhale through the end of the exhale. (Allow for some silence here for as long as you see fit)

5. You may have noticed the mind wandering. When the mind wanders, it offers us an opportunity to cultivate mindfulness and concentration. Each time we notice the mind wandering, we're strengthening our ability to recognize our experience. Each time we bring the mind back to the breath, we're strengthening our ability to focus on an object. Treat it as an opportunity rather than a problem, and return to the breath. (Allow for some silence here for as long as you see fit)

6. You can begin the practice by bringing to mind yourself as you sit here right now. Try to connect with your own deepest intentions for happiness, ease, and safety. You don't need to dive into stories of what will make you happy but connect with that natural desire you have. You can cultivate this intention to open the heart to your wellbeing by silently offering yourself some phrases of Metta. In your head, slowly offer yourself the phrases: "May I be happy." "May I be healthy." "May I be safe." "May I be at ease." You can offer these phrases silently in

your head, saying them slowly enough so that you can connect with their meaning and the intention behind them. (Allow for some silence here for as long as you see fit)

7. You can now bring to mind a good friend. This may be a loved one, a friend, a teacher or mentor, or maybe a pet. You can connect with your natural desire to see this person happy and at ease. Just like you, this person wants to be happy, to feel safe, and to be healthy. To cultivate this intention of kindness, you can offer this person a few phrases of Metta: "May you be happy." "May you be healthy." "May you be safe." "May you be at ease." (Allow for some silence here for as long as you see fit)

8. You can let this person go from your mind and bring to mind a neutral person. This is someone you see, maybe regularly, but don't know very well. It may be somebody who works somewhere you go a lot, a co-worker, or maybe a neighbor. Although you don't know this person well, you can recognize that this person wants to be happy as well. You don't need to know what their happiness looks like necessarily. Again, offer this person the phrases of loving-kindness, connecting to care about their wellbeing. "May you be happy." "May you be healthy." "May you be safe." "May you be at ease." (Allow for some silence here for as long as you see fit)

9. And as you let this neutral person go, you can bring to mind somebody who you find difficult. You may not want to pick the most difficult person in your life, instead choosing someone who is minorly difficult. Maybe it's

someone you find yourself agitated with or annoyed by. Again, offer this person the phrases of loving-kindness, connecting to care about their wellbeing. "May you be happy." "May you be healthy." "May you be safe." "May you be at ease." (Allow for some silence here for as long as you see fit)

Let go of Grudges

This is often easier said than done. But you don't have to do it for the other person. Sometimes, offering forgiveness or dropping a grudge is about compassion towards self and not just for others.

Take some time and assess your relationships with others. Are you harboring any resentment or ill-will toward someone? If so, consider reaching out to them to bury the hatchet. This doesn't have to be a reconciliation. You may just need to end the relationship and move on.

If reaching out isn't an option, try getting your feelings out in a letter. You don't even have to send it to them. Just getting your feelings out of your mind and into the world can be freeing.

Travel Light

Drop your emotional baggage. The burden of our heavy past should be abandoned. Life is a journey and we can't carry everything with us. Only carry the useful stuff.

You've probably heard of the fear of missing out but what about the fear of letting go?

My father was volatile and aggressive. Criticism was his preferred method of communication. As a child and teenager, I learned to keep my thoughts and feelings locked away. Without realizing it, I carried this habit into adulthood, avoiding any talk about my feelings or turning them into a joke. When a friend finally called me on it, the shock of self-recognition quickly turned to resistance. 'This is who I am', I thought. 'Why should I change?'

I trod on, working as hard as ever to keep my fortress intact. It wasn't making me happy yet I wasn't ready to change. As I struggled with my desire to cling to hurtful memories and self-defeating behaviors, it dawned on me that I was afraid to let go because defensiveness was part of my identity.

The problem wasn't that I had baggage—everyone has baggage. The problem was that it had come to define me. I didn't know who I would be without it. At that point, it hit me: I had to dig deep, discover the person I wanted to be, and then act on it.

After I identified that I was holding on to the past because it seemed too important to jettison, I discovered that letting go is harder than it sounds. Relaxing a long-held belief isn't a one-day, one-week, or even a one-year process. However, it is possible.

This is the five-step process you can follow:

1. Write an honest list of the thoughts, beliefs, and behaviours that weigh you down. Grab a pen and notebook, find a quiet space, and spend thirty to forty minutes thinking and writing. It is important, to be honest, and write down whatever comes to mind. Don't judge what comes up, just take note.

2. Reflect on each item and identify the source of the thought. Travel back in time and see where you picked up these items of baggage. Do you fear intimacy because a partner cheated on you? Do you dread the holidays because your parents fought all the time? Acknowledge the painful memories but don't wallow in them. Write them down and move on to the next step.

3. Find at least one positive thing in each hurtful experience. Look for the silver lining in your cloud. For example, my father's criticism made me aware of the power of words and taught me the importance of speaking with kindness. Looking for the good in the past helps you reclaim your power. You are no longer a victim. You decide what you take from that experience.

4. Create affirmations to foster change and counteract negative thoughts. Take the positives from step three

and turn them into affirmations or statements of intent, i.e.: "I will speak with love" or "I will treat people with kindness." This emphasizes positive future behavior and frees you from the past. Make the affirmations tangible: put a reminder on your phone, write them on post-its, or put a list on the fridge.

5. Practice patience and mindfulness. It takes time to change habits, especially when they are rooted in deep hurts or fears. Check-in with yourself regularly using journaling or meditation. If you find yourself shouldering old baggage, be sure to acknowledge it, then gently release it and focus on your affirmations. Replacing negative thoughts with positive actions will help you let go for good.

There are infinite possibilities for each of us, baggage notwithstanding. Everyone has pain. It's part of what makes us who we are. What defines us, however, is how we handle it.

"You can find your identity in the damage that's been done to you. You find your identity in your wounds, in your scars, in the places where you've been beaten up and you turn them into a medal. We all wear the things we've survived with some honor, but the real honor is in also transcending them."

-Bruce Springsteen

By taking the time to identify and understand our baggage and making a conscious decision to let go, we free ourselves to experience life in a richer, deeper, more meaningful way.

Gratitude

Simply being grateful can give your mood a big boost, among other benefits. For example, a recent two-part study done in the psychology department of the Hope College in the USA in 2016, found that practicing gratitude can have a significant impact on feelings of hope and happiness.

Start each day by acknowledging one thing you're grateful for. You can do this while you're brushing your teeth or just waiting for that snoozed alarm to go off again.

As you go about your day, try to keep an eye out for pleasant things in your life. They can be big things, such as knowing that someone loves you or getting a well-deserved promotion. They can also be little things, such as a co-worker who offered you a cup of coffee or the neighbor who waved to you. Maybe even just the warmth of the sun on your skin.

With a little practice, you may even become more aware of all the positive things around you.

Why do we lack Gratitude?

One of the biggest reasons for feeling unhappy or sad is that we don't count our blessings when we wake up every day.

Rather, we focus on the things we lack and believe that our happiness is solely dependent on achieving the next big thing.

We have so many examples in life to prove that happiness from every next physical thing in only short-lived. The moment we get what we are looking for, we again start looking at something bigger than that

If you are consistently focussing on the lack of your life, it will create a never fulfilling mental loop.

"What you focus on grows, what you think about expands and what you dwell upon determines your reality"

-Robin Sharma

You think the glass is half empty. You don't feel grateful that even this half glass can quench your thirst.

One shouldn't make his or her happiness solely dependent on the achievement of the materialistic goals. If you have a house to stay, a vehicle to drive, a reasonable job or a vocation to lead a nice life with your family, you are already better off than a substantial population.

Your gratitude has a positive impact on your future too. Because:

"What you appreciate, appreciates"

-Lynee Twist

What can we appreciate in our day to day life?

1. When you put toothpaste on your toothbrush, think of 1 thing that makes you feel grateful.
2. When you wake up in the morning, glance at a photo that makes you feel happy.
3. think of one good thing from your day at night.

Expressing thanks may be one of the simplest ways to feel better. Gratitude unshackles us from toxic emotions.

In positive psychology research, gratitude is strongly and consistently associated with greater happiness. Gratitude helps people feel more positive emotions, relish good experiences, improve their health, deal with adversity, and build strong relationships.

People feel and express gratitude in multiple ways. They can apply it to the past by retrieving positive memories and being thankful for elements of childhood or past blessings. They can apply it to the present by not taking good fortune for granted as it comes. And they can apply it to the future by maintaining a hopeful and optimistic attitude. Regardless of the inherent or current level of someone's gratitude, it's a quality that individuals can successfully cultivate further.

Ways to cultivate gratitude

Gratitude is a way for people to appreciate what they have instead of always reaching for something new in the hopes it will make them happier, or thinking they can't feel satisfied until every physical and material need is met. Gratitude helps people refocus on what they have instead of what they lack. And, although it may feel contrived at first, this mental state grows stronger with use and practice.

Here are some ways in which you can make the cultivation of gratitude a daily habit.

Write a thank-you note

You can make yourself happier and nurture your relationship with another person by writing a thank-you letter expressing your enjoyment and appreciation of that person's impact on your life. Send it, or better yet, deliver and read it in person if possible. Make a habit of sending at least one gratitude letter a month. Once in a while, write one to yourself.

Thank someone mentally.

No time to write? It may help just to think about someone who has done something nice for you and mentally thank the individual.

Keep a gratitude journal.

Make it a habit to write down or share with a loved one, thoughts about the gifts you've received each day.

Count your blessings.

Pick a time every week to sit down and write about your blessings — reflecting on what went right or what you are grateful for. Sometimes it helps to pick a number — such as three to five things — that you will identify each week. As you write, be specific and think about the sensations you felt when something good happened to you.

Pray

Religious people can use prayer to cultivate gratitude.

Ho'oponopono

Another beautiful technique useful in developing a forgiving heart is 'Ho'oponopono', a powerful Hawaiian forgiveness mantra.
What is Ho'oponopono? And how does it help?

Ho'oponopono is an ancient Hawaiian practise still in use today and is well-known for the miracle it does in clearing negativity from one's mind and thought. It is believed to be designed to wipe out all the negativity in our thoughts and those blocks that are keeping us miserable.

Dr. Joe Vitale is a renowned Ho'oponopono practitioner, He says that there are a large number of us who don't have the luxury of enjoying peace, harmony, or joy forever in our lives. It is believed that external negativity plays a role and we are saddled right from our birth. This Hawaiian technique Ho'oponopono has been specifically designed to remove all the stress and negativity from our minds and let us enjoy eternal happiness. It is a simple technique where you ask for forgiveness and purifies yourself.

There are four phases or steps that we can follow and the magical healing starts from within. The four steps involved in this practice make you realize the fact that you are responsible for everything that happens to you and that is in your mind. Once you realize this fact it becomes easy for you to start practising the steps.

1. The first step asks you to say sorry for everything that has happened or any wrong things that you have witnessed. It makes it easy for you to move ahead in your life once you know the fact and has the courage to say sorry for anything that was wrong, you will feel better.

2. Once you are able to say sorry the second step requires you to ask for forgiveness. You will be seeking forgiveness for everything you felt sorry for in the first step. While doing so you are asking to forgive everything from you and your past memories that may have been involved in the wrongdoing. These may sound weird for many of us but once you mean what you say the process is magical.

3. The third step that you must go through is showing your gratitude for everything that has happened to your life. This way you will learn to appreciate everything that is big or small in your life. You might get an unexpected response for this thank you but you need not worry about the result or response. In right time the correct result will appear in front of you. This step will help you to have patience as well.

4. The last step that you need to follow is to show your love and say I love you to everything that is yours. This way you will learn to love everything related to you.

What's Ho'oponopono theory of magic that will help you can be elaborated further with the effect that each step has on you. It makes you stronger and gives you the courage to face the truth and tell the truth. You will feel better when you know that your request for the forgiveness has been granted and people are going to trust you again. There is no human being on the planet who does not commit sins either knowingly or unknowingly. The ones who dare to see their mistake, and come forward to seek forgiveness are the successful ones. Live your life with no grudges and you will be the happiest person.

There are four sentences to this technique or meditation or prayer whatever you may like to call it. These sentences are so simple that we find it hard to believe in the miracles that they can achieve. Repentance, Forgiveness, Gratitude and Love are the only forces at work here and these forces have amazing power.

The best part of chanting this mantra is that you can do it by yourself. You don't need anyone else to be with you nor do you need anyone to hear you. You can chant the words in your head. The power is in our feeling it and in our willingness to forgive and love.

Chant the following either aloud or in your mind. Chant it for as long as you want to or you can, use a string of 108 beads and chant it while passing the beads through your fingers in the ancient Indian style.

These rather simple but, tremendously powerful words are:

I'M SORRY - PLEASE FORGIVE ME - THANK YOU - I LOVE YOU

The practice makes you love everything that belongs to you. This is important in the sense that people do not tend to care about the things and people that are making their life beautiful. You must show your appreciation for what you have and this will make the bonding stronger. Life is not about yourself but everyone and everything that are connected to you as well. It is necessary you take life as one beautiful chance given to you and handle it with care.

It helps you forget all the bad memories associated with you as you move forward with the forgiveness achieved from your action and prayers. Once you are a regular practitioner of this process you know that life is more about having faith and courage to accept and face the truth. You will never feel the pressure of hiding the bad side of you, rather you will learn to come forward and express what you want to go away from your life. This way you will be living stress-free life with no regrets.

Chapter 4

***

A Way of Life

There are some qualities which you will have to purposefully cultivate and some things you will have to start doing if you wish to make happiness part of your personality.

I have listed some of them below:

Unwavering Faith

The dictionary meaning of Faith is **"a** firm belief in something for which there is no proof" or "something that is believed especially with strong conviction."

The world's top-most strategic coach, Tony Robbins, defines it as "certainty of outcome" in your mind when you are working towards your goals. He states that our success in any venture that we get into, entirely depends on the level of certainty of outcome in our minds, because **only our thinking about the certainty of the outcome will trigger us to produce the quality of actions needed** to get the results.

"Faith is taking the first step, even if you don't see the whole staircase."

–Martin Luther King, Jr.

In addition to a strong belief in our abilities and a growth mindset, we need to develop a deeper sense of complete faith in the goodness of whatever happens in our life. Of course, it doesn't mean that when you have faith or believe strongly in the certainty of the outcome that you expect, you'll always achieve what you desire.

Many uncontrollable factors play a significant role, so despite your best efforts, sometimes you may not get the desired results.

But failures won't steal your happiness because you are already equipped with a growth mindset. **Failure gives you the required experience and prompts you to develop the skill set necessary to handle the situation better.**

Having faith means that, **even if things don't go the way you desired, you believe in the bigger scheme of things. You** believe in the unfolding of life towards a greater good for you. When you have faith, you strongly believe that things don't happen to you; they happen for you.

"Remember that sometimes, not getting what you want is a wonderful stroke of luck."

-Dalai Lama

You know that you can't control your genes or circumstances, but **you can control your actions. You** also realize that as you don't have full control over everything, so you are mindful that your happiness shouldn't solely depend on the outcome. **Your happiness comes from taking action and getting immersed in the activities** rather than overthinking about the past or future.

When you take consistent and massive action**, you invite flow** in your work, and your **happiness is created by your immersion into the activities. So** instead of waiting for some outcome to happen, to make you happier, you immediately experience happiness in the work you do. I'd say it's a win-win proposition. Because if you are joyful and get into the flow of whatever you do, there are great chances that the **quality of your work will be multiple times better than when you are working under stress.**

Finally, the **objective of life is to strive for our goals, because growth is the need of our spirit,but** at the same time, we need to ensure that **we don't tie our momentary happiness to the achievement of those goals.**

Do What You Love

Don't say, "I'll do what I love after I retire." Instead, plan on spending some time now, doing things you love. Even if it's a simple hobby. Decide when you can devote a little time regularly. If you don't like the work you're doing now, maybe you should consider a change of career.

When you find an activity that you enjoy, one that challenges you, and increases your skill, you'll find yourself fully engaged in it. You'll be in a flow state. This means you'll be concentrating on the present and may even lose your sense of time. This feels good and contributes to your well-being and happiness.

Reframe Obstacles

No one gets through life without encountering obstacles. So, each time an obstacle pops up, try to reframe it as a challenge that you can handle. If you need support, think of a time when you surmounted your fear and successfully took action. Be a problem solver. You may ask yourself, 'How can I fix this?' Questioning opens the creative parts of your brain and you may come up with more than one solution. If life gives you a lemon, make lemonade.

Random Acts of Kindness

Practising acts of kindness gives people a happiness boost. Besides, the recipient becomes happier and this even extends to people who merely observe the act.

These acts could be anything from giving a smile, helping someone cross the road to gifting something handmade to a friend or loved one. It could also be assisting a family member with household chores. So please do more acts of kindness to make the world a happier place.

People perform acts of kindness both to do good and to feel good. Research finds that being kind makes us happy, helps to lower our blood pressure, and encourages stronger social connections. Now, a new study suggests that we can access some of these benefits simply by recalling acts of kindness we did in the past—making kindness a gift that keeps on giving.

Give a compliment. That's a beautiful act of kindness which does not cost you anything. Giving a sincere compliment is a quick, easy way to brighten someone's day while giving your own happiness a boost. Catch the person's eye and say it with a smile so they know you mean it. You might be surprised by how good it makes you feel. If you want to offer someone a compliment on their physical appearance, make sure to do it respectfully.

Practice 'Mudita'

'Mudita' means Sympathetic Joy. It is an important component of the Buddha's teachings. Mudita is taking sympathetic or altruistic joy in observance of the happiness of others. Mudita is the ability to take active delight in others' good fortune or good deeds as a way to develop and maintain calmness of mind. People also identify Mudita with empathy. The antithesis of Mudita is jealousy and envy which makes you unhappy.

By being happy when good things happen to others, your opportunities for delight are greatly increased. Practice Mudita when you observe the success and happiness in others.

Look your best

Dress well, be well-groomed, take frequent showers. Happy clothes include well-cut, figure-enhancing items made from bright and beautiful fabrics. Wear fancy jewellery, good quality makeup, splash on your favourite perfume. Men, do have a good haircut. Shave your beard or trim it. Have a manicure and a pedicure.

Recreation

Take up a hobby When it comes to improving your mental health, there are few better remedies than picking up a healthy hobby. Hobbies can get your mind active, and get you social—but the real benefit to most people is the boost to overall mental wellness. No matter what sort of mental issue you're struggling with, there's a good chance that throwing yourself into a hobby will have a positive effect on you. Listen to music, sing loudly even if it is in your bathroom, dance even if you are alone.

Our daily lives are filled with stress—from our jobs, our kids, school, bills, and relationship conflict to a seemingly endless list of other minor stressors. Hobbies play an important role in mitigating some of this unavoidable stress, as they provide us with an outlet for creativity, distraction, and something to look forward to.

Hobbies bring a sense of fun and freedom to life that can help to minimize the impact of chronic stress. Those who feel overwhelmed at a job, for example, can benefit from hobbies because they provide an outlet for stress and something to look forward to after a hard day or week at a stressful job.

Having a hobby to focus on forces us to take a break from stressful activities. Without a reason to take a break, we may unwittingly overwork ourselves to the point of exhaustion. Studies have shown that some of the best hobbies for reducing stress include knitting, gardening, reading, quilting, painting singing dancing and the list goes on.

Join a laughter yoga club

Laughter Yoga Clubs are social clubs that are free for all, anywhere in the world. Laughter Yoga is like an aerobic exercise (cardio workout) which brings more oxygen to the body and brain which makes one feel healthier and more energetic. Laughter Yoga strengthens the immune system.

In India, most Laughter Clubs function on a daily basis and the members meet at public parks where people go for a morning walk. If you want to start a Laughter Club, find a place in your locality where people can assemble early morning while going for a walk. The concept of Laughter Clubs is slightly different in the West where club members like to meet for 1-2 hours every weekend or fortnightly. They laugh together for 30 minutes along with breathing and stretching exercises, followed by Laughter Meditation for 30 mins.

Back to Nature

We all know how good being in nature can make us feel. We have known it for centuries. The sounds of the forest, the scent of the trees, the sunlight playing through the leaves, the fresh, clean air — these things give us a sense of comfort. They ease our stress and worry, help us to relax and to think more clearly. Being in nature can restore our mood, give us back our energy and vitality, refresh and rejuvenate us.

Sometimes when I'm in the shower I imagine I'm washing away all my stress, negative feelings, sadness, remorse and anger. When I'm in the bathtub I imagine I'm soaking up love, appreciation warmth kindness care etc. When I bask in the sun, I imagine the sun is pouring joy, health prosperity etc on me. When I walk barefoot on the ground, I imagine drawing strength, stability and energy from the earth.

Nature therapy sometimes referred to as ecotherapy, describes a broad group of techniques or treatments intending to improve an individual's mental or physical health, specifically with an individual's presence within nature or outdoor surroundings. One example of nature therapy is forest bathing or 'shinrin-yoku', a practice that combines a range of exercises and tasks in an outdoor environment.

If you're looking to reduce the stress of city life, escape to the forest and talk to the trees.

Concrete jungles create a lot of stress in our lives, which is why more and more people are turning to the gifts of nature for therapy — like tree-hugging, walking barefoot on the grass, mud or sand.

Hugging a tree increases levels of the hormone oxytocin. This hormone is responsible for feeling calm and emotional bonding. When hugging a tree, the hormones serotonin and dopamine make you feel happier. It is important to use this "free" space of a forest we were given by nature to holistically heal ourselves.

Life on earth is unimaginable without the Sun. Natural light is crucial for our health and well-being. The sunlight helps to regulate the natural rhythms of our body and not getting enough of it can impact our health in surprising ways. Exposure to sun rays also called sunbath therapy has been in use from ancient times due to its disease-fighting properties. Let's know what are the benefits of the sunbath.

Sunrays have several healing powers. They not only heal you physically but also emotionally. Remember the song by John Denver- Sunshine on my shoulders makes me happy. Breath Fresh air as often as you can. Try to drink natural spring water whenever you get a chance.

Face stress head-on

Life is full of stressors, and it's impossible to avoid all of them. For those stressors you can't avoid, remind yourself that everyone has stress — there's no reason to think it's all on you. And chances are, you're stronger than you think you are. Instead of letting yourself get overwhelmed, try to tackle the stressor head-on. This might mean initiating an uncomfortable conversation or putting in some extra work, but the sooner you tackle it, the sooner the pit in your stomach will start to shrink.

Look at Life as an Adventure

"Do not stop thinking of life as an adventure."
-Eleanor Roosevelt

Finally, if you think life as an adventure, you'll enjoy all the challenges coming in the way. Instead of avoiding, you'll move forward to seek those challenges.

Five Happiness Affirmations

'It's the repetition of affirmations that leads to belief. And once that belief becomes a deep conviction, things begin to happen.'

– Muhammad Ali

1. "The Universe Supports Me."

When you're feeling low or alone, it can be hard to feel as though anyone is on your side. This affirmation is a great reminder that you are never alone and that despite how things may seem, life is always on your side. The universe is continually orchestrating for things to work in your favour. You should keep having faith and your mind fixed firmly on what it is that you want most. Understand that these affirmations are going to become a reality for you.

2. "I Am Enough."

You are enough, exactly as you are right now. When you feel the pressures of life crashing down on you or you believe that happiness is only possible once you've achieved this, or look like that, it's time to bring yourself back to a place of self-love and know that you are always, already, enough.

3. "My Heart Is Always Open and I Radiate Love."

Whether you're struggling with relationship problems, low self-esteem, work stresses or whatever it may be; you will always find that the best solution is rooted in love. So, use this as a reminder to always keep your heart open to giving and receiving love in all its forms.

4. "I Have Everything I Need to Be Happy Right Now."

Gratitude is the most powerful tool there is for immediate, inner happiness. So, no matter what's going on around you, with this affirmation take a moment to reflect on everything you have to be grateful for and capture this feeling to see you through the rest of your day.

5. "My Dreams Are Coming True Every Day."

Use these affirmations upon waking up or the last thing at night, remind yourself of this until it becomes an integrated part of you.

A few more Affirmations for Happiness

1. I choose to be happy and grateful today.

2. Happiness flows through me constantly.

3. My future is full of light and laughter.

4. There are amazing things in my life; no matter how small they may seem, they are significant.

5. I am at peace with my past.

Chapter 5

***

An Inwards Journey

<u>Meditation</u>

You've probably heard that meditation can reduce stress, boost your immune system, and make you a happier, more focused person. But there are so many types of meditations, it can be hard to know which one will meet your needs.

What is meditation?

Meditation is an approach to training the mind, similar to the way that fitness is an approach to training the body.

Meditation is exploring. It's not a fixed destination. Your head doesn't become vacuumed free of thought immediately. It's a special place where each moment is momentous. When we meditate we venture into the workings of our minds: our sensations (air blowing on our skin or a harsh smell wafting into the room), our emotions (love this, hate that, crave this, loathe that) and thoughts (wouldn't it be weird to see an elephant playing the trumpet).

Many meditation techniques exist — so how do you learn how to meditate? It's extremely difficult for a beginner to sit for hours and think of nothing or have an "empty mind." However, there are plenty of meditation techniques for us to choose from.

The first step to starting a regular meditation practice is finding the style of meditation that's right for you. There are plenty of styles for you to choose from. You can try some of them and see which one suits you best. I have bellowed some of the techniques which I found helpful.

Where ever there are steps, script or instructions given for meditation in this book, you can either read out loud and record in your voice and play it. Or you could ask someone to read it for you. You can also go to my YouTube channel and play the audio.

Anapana Sati Meditation

This one is my favourite. This is the meditation practice followed by the Buddha to attain Nirvana or Enlightenment. This entails following the breath as we inhale and exhale. Breathing is something we do involuntarily as well as we can do it voluntarily that's why it is considered as the bridge between the conscious and the subconscious mind. If you do this with concentration and consistently, we can go to the alpha state. The alpha state of mind is when you reach a very relaxed state while awake. Another benefit of this meditation is that you can do it anytime and anywhere. 'Anapana Sati' makes you calm and aware.

Tratak Meditation

This meditation requires you to focus on a single point. staring at a candle flame, at the rising or the setting sun, a star, a dot, an idol etc. Since focusing the mind is challenging, a beginner might meditate for only a few minutes and then work up to longer durations. You simply refocus your awareness on the chosen object of attention each time you notice your mind wandering. Through this process, your ability to concentrate improves.

Mindfulness meditation

Mindfulness meditation asks us to suspend judgment and unleash our natural curiosity about the workings of the mind, approaching our experience with warmth and kindness, to ourselves and others.

Mindfulness meditation encourages the practitioner to observe wandering thoughts as they drift through the mind. The intention is not to get involved with the thoughts or to judge them, but simply to be aware of each mental note as it arises.

Through mindfulness meditation, you can see how your thoughts and feelings tend to move in particular patterns. Over time, you can become more aware of the human tendency to quickly judge an experience as good or bad, pleasant or unpleasant. With practice, an inner balance develops. What is mindfulness?

Mindfulness is the basic human ability to be fully present, aware of where we are and what we're doing, and not overly reactive or overwhelmed by what's going on around us.

While mindfulness is something, we all naturally possess, it's more readily available to us when we practice daily.

Whenever you bring awareness to what you're directly experiencing via your senses, or to your state of mind via your thoughts and emotions, you're being mindful. And there's growing research showing that when you train your brain to be mindful, you're remodelling the physical structure of your brain.

The goal of mindfulness is to wake up to the inner workings of our mental, emotional, and physical processes.

How do I practice mindfulness and meditation?

Mindfulness is available to us in every moment, whether through meditations and body scans, or mindful moment practises like taking time to pause and breathe when the phone rings instead of rushing to answer it.

Vipassana

Satyanarayan Goenka teaches a meditation technique given by the Buddha. It involves observing the sensations on the body. He calls it Vipassana. They have 10-day courses at their centres all over the world where this meditation is taught free of cost, step-by-step each day. These centres run on the generous donations given as gratitude by ex-students who have benefited hugely from these courses. You can enrol yourself at www.dhamma.org

I'm not writing down the steps here because it is best to learn from a teacher trained by S.N. Goenka.

Progressive Muscle Relaxation (PMR)

Steps to Practice Progressive Muscle Relaxation

Find a quiet place free from distractions. Lie on the floor or recline in a chair, loosen any tight clothing, and remove glasses or contacts. Rest your hands in your lap or on the arms of the chair. Take a few slow even breaths.

Now, focus your attention on the following areas, being careful to leave the rest of your body relaxed.

Forehead.

Squeeze the muscles in your forehead, holding for 15 seconds. Feel the muscles becoming tighter and tenser. Then, slowly release the tension in your forehead while counting for 30 seconds. Notice the difference in how your muscles feel and the sensation of relaxation. Continue to release the tension until your forehead feels completely relaxed. Continue breathing slowly and evenly.

Jaw.

Tense the muscles in your jaw, holding for 15 seconds. Then release the tension slowly while counting for 30 seconds.

Notice the feeling of relaxation and continue to breathe slowly and evenly.

Neck and shoulders.

Increase tension in your neck and shoulders by raising your shoulders toward your ears and hold for 15 seconds. Slowly release the tension as you count for 30 seconds. Notice the tension melting away.

Arms and hands.

Slowly draw both hands into fists. Pull your fists into your chest and hold for 15 seconds, squeezing as tight as you can. Then slowly release while you count for 30 seconds. Notice the feeling of relaxation.

Buttocks.

Slowly increase tension in your buttocks over 15 seconds. Then, slowly release the tension over 30 seconds. Notice the tension melting away. Continue to breathe slowly and evenly.

Legs.

Slowly increase the tension in your quadriceps and calves over 15 seconds. Squeeze the muscles as hard as you can. Then gently release the tension over 30 seconds. Notice the tension melting away and the feeling of relaxation that is left.

Feet.

Slowly increase the tension in your feet and toes. Tighten the muscles as much as you can. Then slowly release the tension while you count for 30 seconds. Notice all the tension melting away. Continue breathing slowly and evenly.

Enjoy the feeling of relaxation sweeping through your body. Continue to breathe slowly and evenly. This technique works well when you feel stressed and want to relax

Lake, Mountain, and TreeMeditations by Jon Kabat Zinn

Visualisations play a vital role in enriching and deepening your meditative experience. A good thing about visualisation is that one can be in any posture or be doing one's daily activities and yet enter into a meditative experience.

Jon Kabat-Zinn has introduced many such visualisation tools that we can make instrumental in enhancing our meditative experience.

Mountain Meditation

Mountains elementally rock solid that represents a resolute determination to a practitioner of meditation. Like mountains sore the skies and yet are deeply rooted into the ground that they stand upon, so too, a practitioner can

progress in her practice and yet be rooted in the fragile but tenacious reality of one's life. But this fragility is exactly what, with a strong determination like a firm and stable mountain, a practitioner is determined to transcend. Jon Kabat-Zinn in his beautiful technique teaches us how to borrow the qualities of a mountain in resolving to ourselves in bringing an inner change with a quintessentially emblematic quality of a mountain of abiding presence and stillness.

Instructions

This meditation is normally done in a sitting position, either on the floor or a chair, and begins by sensing into the support you have from the chair or the cushion, paying attention to the actual sensations of contact. Finding a position of stability and poise, upper body balanced over your hips and shoulders in a comfortable but alert posture, hands on your lap or your knees, arms hanging by their own weight, like heavy curtains, stable and relaxed.

Actually, sensing into your body, feeling your feet... legs... hips... lower and upper body... arms... shoulders... neck... head...

And when you are ready, allowing your eyes to close, bringing awareness to the breath, the actual physical sensations, feeling each breath as it comes in and goes out... letting the breath be just as it is, without trying to change or regulate it in any way... allowing it to flow easily and naturally, with its own rhythm and pace, knowing you are breathing perfectly well right now, nothing for you to do...

Allowing the body to be still and sitting with a sense of dignity, a sense of resolve, a sense of being complete, whole, in this very moment, with your posture reflecting this sense of wholeness... (long pause)

As you sit here, letting an image form in your mind's eye, of the most magnificent or beautiful mountain you know or have seen or can imagine..., letting it gradually come into greater focus... and even if it doesn't come as a visual image, allowing the sense of this mountain and feeling its overall shape, its lofty peak or peaks high in the sky, the large base rooted in the bedrock of the earth's crust, it's steep or gently sloping sides...

Noticing how massive it is, how solid, how unmoving, how beautiful, whether from afar or up close...(pause)

Perhaps your mountain has snow blanketing its top and trees reaching down to the base, or rugged granite sides... there may be streams and waterfalls cascading down the slopes... there may be one peak or a series of peaks, or with meadows and high lakes...

Observing it, noting its qualities and when you feel ready, seeing if you can bring the mountain into your own body sitting here so that your body and the mountain in your mind's eye become one so that as you sit here, you share in the massiveness and the stillness and majesty of the mountain, you become the mountain.

Grounded in the sitting posture, your head becomes the lofty peak, supported by the rest of the body and affording a panoramic view. Your shoulders and arms the sides of the mountain. Your buttocks and legs the solid base, rooted to your cushion or your chair, experiencing in your body a sense of uplift from deep within your pelvis and spine.

With each breath, as you continue sitting, becoming a little more a breathing mountain, alive and vital, yet unwavering in your inner stillness, completely what you are, beyond words and thoughts, a centred, grounded, unmoving presence...

As you sit here, becoming aware of the fact that as the sun travels across the sky, the light and shadows and colours are changing virtually moment by moment in the mountain's stillness, and the surface teems with life and activity... streams, melting snow, waterfalls, plants and wildlife.

As the mountain sits, seeing and feeling how night follows day and day follows night. The bright warming sun, followed by the cool night sky studded with stars, and the gradual dawning of a new day...

Through it all, the mountain just sits, experiencing the change in each moment, constantly changing, yet always just being itself. It remains still as the seasons flow into one another and as the weather changes moment by moment and day by day, calmness abiding all change...

In summer, there is no snow on the mountain except perhaps for the very peaks or in crags shielded from direct sunlight

In the fall, the mountain may wear a coat of brilliant fire colours.

In winter, a blanket of snow and ice.

In any season, it may find itself at times enshrouded in clouds or fog or pelted by freezing rain. People may come to see the mountain and comment on how beautiful it is or how it's not a good day to see the mountain, that it's too cloudy or rainy or foggy or dark.

None of these matter to the mountain, which remains at all times its essential self. Clouds may come and clouds may go, tourists may like it or not. The mountain's magnificence and beauty are not changed one bit by whether people see it or not, seen or unseen, in sun or clouds, broiling or frigid, day or night.

It just sits, being itself.

At times visited by violent storms, buffeted by snow and rain and winds of unthinkable magnitude.

Through it all, the mountain sits.

Spring comes, trees leaf out, flowers bloom in the high meadows and slopes, birds sing in the trees once again. Streams overflow with the waters of melting snow.

Through it all, the mountain continues to sit, unmoved by the weather, by what happens on its surface, by the world of appearances… remaining its essential self, through the seasons, the changing weather, the activity ebbing and flowing on its surface…

In the same way, as we sit in meditation, we can learn to experience the mountain, we can embody the same central, unwavering stillness and groundedness in the face of everything that changes in our own lives, over seconds, over hours, over years.

In our lives and our meditation practise, we experience constantly the changing nature of mind and body and the outer world, we have our periods of light and darkness, activity and inactivity, our moments of colour and our moments of drabness.

We indeed experienced storms of varying intensity and violence in the outer world and our minds and bodies, buffeted by high winds, by cold and rain, we endure periods of darkness and pain, as well as the moments of joy and uplift, even our appearance changes constantly, experiencing weather of its own...

By becoming the mountain in our meditation practice, we can link up with its strength and stability and adopt them for our own. We can use its energies to support our energy to encounter each moment with mindfulness and equanimity and clarity.

It may help us to see that our thoughts and feelings, our preoccupations, our emotional storms and crises, even the things that happen to us are very much like the weather on the mountain. We tend to take it all personally, but its strongest characteristic is impersonal.

The weather of our own lives is not be ignored or denied, it is to be encountered, honoured, felt, known for what it is, and held in awareness... And in holding it in this way, we come to know a deeper silence and stillness and wisdom.

Mountains have this to teach us and much more if we can let it in...

So if you find you resonate in some way with the strength and stability of the mountain in your sitting, it may be helpful to use it from time to time in your meditation practice, to remind you of what it means to sit mindfully with resolve and with wakefulness, in true stillness…

Continuing to sustain the mountain meditation on your own, in silence, moment by moment, for as long as you are comfortable.

Lake Meditation

Lake as a body of flowing water has a serenity to it. It also has a lot of vibrance which is undisturbed by any obstacle that comes its way. Water is as elemental as a rock but is stronger because it wears down the rock.

When we talk about overcoming obstacles, we are primarily talking about the thoughts that our mind is crowded with, while we meditate. Our mind should be like Water exhibiting the quality of taking in this 'information' and yet be in a continuous resuming mode showing our determination of overcoming this obstacle and staying our ground. A strong determination, a continuous flow in ourselves, is what will give us results in our meditational endeavour.

Script

This meditation is done mainly in a lying or reclining position, and begins by paying attention to the actual sensations of contact and support as you lie down, noticing where your body is making contact, how your weight is distributed on the floor, bed or recliner… sensing into your body, feeling your feet… your legs… hips… lower and upper body… arms… your shoulders and your head…

And when you are ready, bringing awareness to the breath, the actual physical sensations, feeling each breath as it comes in and goes out… letting the breath be just as it is, without trying to change or regulate it in any way… allowing it to flow easily and naturally, with its own rhythm and pace, knowing you are breathing perfectly well right now, nothing for you to do, allowing a sense of being complete, whole, in this very moment, just letting your breath be your breath…

As you rest here, letting an image form in your mind's eye of a lake, a body of water, large or small, held in a receptive basin by the earth itself, noting in the mind's eye and your own heart, that water likes to pool in low places, it seeks its own level, asks to be held, contained.

Letting this image gradually come into greater focus. Even if it doesn't come as a visual image, allowing the sense of this lake and feeling its presence…

The lake you're invoking may be deep or shallow, blue or green, muddy or clear. With no wind, the surface will be flat, mirror-like, reflecting trees rocks, sky and clouds, holding everything in itself momentarily…

Wind may come and stir up waves, causing the reflections to distort and disappear, but then sunlight may sparkle in the ripples and dance on the waves in a play of shimmering diamonds…

When night comes, it's the moon's turn to dance on the lake, or when the surface is still, to be reflected in it along with the outline of trees and shadows. In winter, the lake may freeze over, yet be teeming with movement and life below...

As you rest here breathing, as you establish this image of a lake in your mind's eye, allowing yourself, when you feel ready, to bring it inside yourself completely, so that your being merges with the lake, becomes one with it, so that all your energies in this moment are held in awareness with openness and compassion for yourself, in the same way as the lake's waters are held by the receptive and accepting basin of the earth herself.

Breathing as the lake, feeling its body as your body, allowing your mind and your heart to be open and receptive, moment by moment, to reflect whatever comes near, or to be clear all the way to the bottom. Experiencing moments of complete stillness, when both reflection and water are completely clear...and other moments perhaps when the surface is disturbed, choppy, stirred up, reflections and depth lost for the moment.

And through it all, as you lie here, simply observing the play of the various energies of your mind and heart, the fleeting thoughts and feelings, impulses and reactions, which come and go as ripples and waves, noting their effects. In contact with them, just as you are in contact with and feel the various changing energies that play on the lake, the wind, the waves, the light, the shadows and the reflections, the colours and smells.

Noticing the effect of your thoughts and feelings. Do they disturb the surface and clarity of the mind's lake? Do they muddy the waters? Is that okay with you? Isn't having a rippling or a wavy surface a part of being a lake? Might it be possible to identify not only with the surface of your lake but with the entire body of water, so that you become the stillness below the surface as well, which at most experiences only gentle undulations, even when the surface is choppy and ragged?

And in the same way, in your meditation practice and your daily life, can you be in touch, not only with the changing content and intensity of your thoughts and feelings but also with the vast unwavering reservoir of awareness itself, residing below the surface of your mind. The lake can teach this, remind us of the lake within ourselves.

If you find this image to be of value, you may want to use it from time to time to deepen and enrich your meditation practice. You might also invite this lake image to empower you and guide your actions in the world as you move through the unfolding of each day, carrying this vast reservoir of mindfulness within your heart...

Dwelling here in the stillness of this moment, until signalled by the sound of the bells, we can be the lake in silence now, affirming our ability to hold in awareness and acceptance, right now, all our qualities of mind and body, just as the lake sits held, cradled, contained by the earth, reflecting sun, moon, stars, trees, clouds and sky, birds and light, caressed by the air and the wind, which bring out and highlight its sparkle, its vitality, its potential, moment by moment.

Continue to sustain the lake meditation on your own for as long as you are comfortable, in silence, moment by moment, being the lake with its storms and moments of peace.

Tree Meditation

Standing meditation is best learned from trees. If possible, stand close to one or under it. If not stand anywhere you find convenient. Feel your feet developing roots into the ground. Feel your body sway gently, as it always will, just as trees do in a breeze. Staying put, in touch with your breathing, drink in what is in front of you, or keep your eyes closed and sense your surroundings. Sense the tree closest to you. Listen to it, feel its presence, touch it with your mind and body.

Use your breath to help you to stay in the moment...feeling your own body standing, breathing, being, moment by moment.

When mind or body first signals that perhaps it is time to move on, stay with the standing a while longer, remembering that trees stand still for years, occasionally lifetimes if they are fortunate. See if they do not have something to teach you about stillness and about being in touch. After all, they are touching the ground with roots and trunk, the air with trunk and branches, sunlight and the wind with their leaves; everything about a standing tree speaks of being in touch. Experiment with standing this way yourself, even for short periods. Work at being in touch with the air on your skin, the feel of the feet in contact with the ground, the sounds of the world, the dance of light and colour and shadow, the dance of the mind.

Standing like this wherever you find yourself, in the woods, in the mountains, by a river, in your living room, or just waiting for the bus. When you are alone, you might try opening your palms to the sky and holding your arms out in various positions, like branches and leaves, accessible, open, receptive, patient.

Thich Nhat Hanh's Walking Meditation

One of the strongest supporters of walking meditation, Thich Nhat Hanh says that every path, every street in the world is your walking meditation path. Walking meditation is practising meditation while walking. It can bring you joy and peace while you practice it.

Take short steps in complete relaxation; go slowly with a smile on your lips, with your heart open to an experience of peace. You can feel truly at ease with yourself. Your steps can be those of the healthiest, most secure person on earth. All sorrows and worries can drop away while you are walking. To have peace of mind, to attain self-liberation, learn to walk in this way. It is not difficult. You can do it. Anyone can do it who has some degree of mindfulness and a true intention to be happy.

There are varied forms of Walking Meditation out there like, Theravada Walking Meditation, Zen Walking Meditation, Mindfulness Walking Meditation, Yoga Walking Meditation, and Daoist Walking Meditation but, Thich Nhat Hanh's technique stands out for its simplicity in application.

Script

Walk slowly, with calmness and comfort

Be aware of each move, of each step. Keep bringing your attention to the present moment.

Mentally repeat one of these verses, as you walk

Breathing in "I have arrived"; Breathing out "I am home"

Breathing in "In the here"; Breathing out "In the now"

Breathing in "I am solid"; Breathing out "I am free"

Breathing in "In the ultimate"; Breathing out "I dwell"

Enjoy every step you take. Kiss the earth with your feet, imprinting gratitude and love as you walk.

Creative Visualization

What Is Creative Visualization?

Creative visualization is using the power of our mind to imagine the desired outcome. This meditation can be used to promote success in every area of our lives. Visualization is the process of putting together visual mental imagery of what you are wanting to manifest. Consequently, you can start to gain emotions associated with the desired image. In simpler terms, creative visualization is where you visualize what you want and experience the emotions or feelings you would have if it were true.

This can then help you to put your goals and desires out into the universe and start to feel motivated to achieve them. Much like a vision board, but the imagery is in your mind, not physical, although both creative visualization and a physical vision board have very similar purposes.

Creative Visualization can be extremely powerful as you are using the mind's eye to create detailed images of what you want to manifest. This can help you to feel more positive and motivated to achieve these goals. After visualizing, you should feel inspired and ready to take action towards your goals.

If you are constantly repeating certain thoughts to yourself, your subconscious mind accepts these thoughts and this causes a change in your long-term mindset.

This change in mindset can then have a knock-on effect on your behaviours, feelings, and habits. And this is the reason why creative visualization can be so effective!

The mind is a very powerful thing and the visual images that are created through creative visualization can determine some of the strong feelings and emotions that you experience when you think of them. This is why it's important to be clear about what you want to visualize and why.

You can use creative visualization to help you achieve and manifest the outcomes that you desire. These thoughts can be repeated in your mind, which should help to change your mindset and ultimately, your behaviour, in a way that is geared towards your goals.

Lastly, creative visualization can also be used for a therapeutic application. This is where visual imagery can be used to replace and recreate images that are upsetting or cause stress.

Benefits of Creative Visualization Techniques

Now that you know the basics of what visualization is, let's take a deeper look at the benefits. Creative Visualization techniques can offer many benefits and it can do much more than just help you with your manifestations.

Here are 6 benefits of Creative Visualization techniques.

1. Busts Stress

Creative Visualization has shown that positive visual mental images help to increase physical and mental relaxation and decrease stress. Even just taking the time out of your day to be still, silent and relaxed when visualizing can help to reduce your stress and help you feel more positive. Visualization is a form of relaxation just like any other meditation.

Because you would normally be visualizing positive situations, it can naturally help to quieten your mind and keep you feeling relaxed.

2. Develops Focus

You can increase your focus and concentration by sitting down and visualizing. When you perform a task such as creative visualization you are forgetting your troubles from the day and any worries you might have about the future. This gives you a chance to just focus and concentrate on your visualizations.

3. Gain Self Confidence

When you visualize, you are normally picturing yourself achieving success and experiencing positive situations. This means that your self-confidence can increase, as you would be starting to believe in yourself and that your visualizations could come true. The more you visualize yourself doing amazing things, the more confident in yourself you can become.

4. Brings You Joy

Even though the visualization may not be true right now, even the thought of it can spark joy in your life. This is because your mind won't know the difference between the visualization and doing that thing.

This means that you can experience the joy and excitement you would feel if it were real, which only makes your visualizations stronger.

5. Gives You Inspiration

Just like with our confidence, visualizations can also give us a big dose of inspiration. When we visualize our goals and dreams, we become inspired to make them happen. This inspiration can spur us to take action toward our goals.

If we can see our goals in a visualization then it inspires us to make sure we will see it in our reality as well.

6. Improved Relationships

As creative visualization can help you with positivity, motivation, confidence, and inspiration, it can also help you with improved relationships. This could be with friends or a partner.

As you visualize you become more confident in yourself and your abilities. This can help to improve your social life and relationships as your overall wellbeing will be improved.

Six Steps to Begin Using Creative Visualization

Are you looking for your dream job? Or maybe you are on the search for a suitable partner or wondering how you can develop more self-confidence... Now you know the reasons to start using visualization in your manifestation practice, we can take a deeper delve into how to use creative visualization in practice.

Whatever your goal, be sure to try these basic steps to start using creative visualization to your advantage.

Step One: Set the Mood

It is vital to be in a relaxed and positive state of mind when you attempt creative visualization. For example, you might try taking a quiet walk in a peaceful area, soaking in a hot bath or listening to mellow instrumental music.

Once you're feeling relaxed, find a place where you won't be disturbed and can be comfortable for the duration of the process. The longer you can spend working on your visualization, the more effective it is likely to be.

Step Two: Enter A Meditative State

Creative visualization tends to be most intense and meaningful if you take the time to do a straightforward meditative exercise before you begin. For most people, all that is needed is a few minutes spent focusing on slow, steady breathing.

Step Three: Visualize Your Goal

Once your mind feels still and receptive, start crafting an image of the thing you want, taking as long as you like to build up all of the details.

For example, if you are working towards a major promotion at work, imagine yourself receiving the announcement and picture the positive reactions of people around you.

Try to make the environment as realistic as possible, and do your best to experience not just the sights but also the sounds, scents and tactile sensations associated with your goal.

Step Four: Hold onto The Feelings Associated with Your Visualization

Although the most important part of creative visualization is the process described in step three, you are more likely to see your goals manifest in your life if you allow your visualization experiences to influence the rest of your day.

Try to hold onto the feelings of pride, happiness, confidence, and peace that you experience when you picture your goal, and repeatedly affirm your belief that you will soon attract the things you yearn for.

Step Five: Make A Habit of Using Creative Visualization

Ideally, you should make creative visualization a daily part of your life. Most people find it useful to set aside a specific time for the visualization (such as fifteen minutes before going to sleep), but the most important thing is that you maintain your ritual of visualizing your goal until you obtain what you want in your life.

Step Six: Work Hard to Achieve Your Goal

Although creative visualization is incredibly powerful and can certainly play a huge role in allowing you to develop the life you've always wanted, you substantially increase your chances of success if you also take concrete steps towards your goals.

Take every relevant opportunity you encounter, be brave, and believe in a happier, more fulfilling life.

You can try all of these methods, and choose one which suits you best. Once you have made a choice practise it daily for at least for ninety days to see significant results.

Chapter 6

***

Happy Mind in a Healthy Body

Exercise

Physical Exercise isn't just for your body. Exercise helps in reducing anxiety, stress and feelings of depression. It has proved to boost, self-esteem, self-confidence, and of course happiness.

Even a small amount of physical activity can bring a huge transformation if done regularly. The trick is not to overexert. If you abruptly start strenuous exercise, you might end up frustrated and sore and eventually give up.

To begin with, you may consider:

1. Going for a walk in the neighbourhood every night after dinner.
2. Dancing to your favourite music.
3. Starting your day with pranayama or yoga.

Think of any physical activity you used to enjoy doing but have stooped now. Now would be a great time to restart. Or think of something physical you always wanted to do or learn like climbing a mountain or swimming. Do it now. It's never too late.

"To keep the body in good health is a duty otherwise we shall not be able to keep the mind strong and clear"

-Buddha

Exercise makes you feel happy and energetic. It's a major component of a healthy and h.appy life. Not only does it burn off calories, but makes the muscles firmer, redistributes the bodyweight and improves posture. With exercise not only will you look and feel healthier and sleep better, but will find that you are more energetic and alert and less prone to depression. Exercise also helps prevent many diseases, such as cancer, heart attack, heart disease, diabetes and controls blood sugar and blood pressure. It lowers stress and promotes weight loss. In today's world of multi-tasking, we go through immense stress. Some of us can cope up mainly due to our good health, however, the majority of us are pulled down to such an extent that it takes a toll on our bodies and mind along with that, exercise also improves the immune system. It can fulfil a dream everyone dreams of that is "Slowing down the ageing process".

"True enjoyment comes from the activity of the mind and exercise of the body, the two are ever united"

-Wilhelm von Humboldt

Lack of exercise makes one sluggish and feel exhausted, while exercise makes you feel energetic and renewed.

"The purpose of training is to tighten the slack, toughen the body and polish the spirit"

-Morihei Ueshiba

Various forms of Exercises

"Training gives us an outlet for suppressed energies created by stress and thus tones the spirit just as exercise conditions the body"

-Arnold Schwarzenegger

To enable to choose the appropriate form of exercise, information on various forms and their benefits are given below:

Yoga

Yoga is a means of balancing and harmonizing the body, mind and emotions. It combines low-impact exercise with stretching and breathing. Yoga is different from most of the other forms of exercise in that, it is not concerned with how many repetitions are performed or how well a person performs a particular exercise. Instead, yoga focuses your attention on how your body is structured and how to move without aggravating any injury or causing pain. It teaches you to breathe properly and to integrate breathing with the positions of the body. You don't strain or force your body when doing yoga, rather it gently stretches various muscles. It improves strength, flexibility and endurance. There are several types of yoga, Hatha Yoga is popular. Power Yoga has also become popular in recent years. It is generally preferred by athletes to develop strength and stamina.

Aerobic Exercise

Aerobic means "in the presence of air". It's a kind of exercise that gets you breathing deeply and more rapidly than normal. Aerobic exercises generally work on the large muscle groups of the body in repetitive motions for a sustained period of time. Walking, jogging, cycling, skipping, swimming, dancing are all forms of aerobic exercises.

Walking

Walking is the simplest way to improve health. Walking improves the circulation, stimulates the heart and lungs, loosens the joints and helps walker lose weight. Walking does not involve any violent exertion and hence has no side effects. On the contrary, it has the advantage of being something that can be done every day, and by almost anyone, regardless of age and state of health. If you have not been walking regularly and need company, get a partner and start walking. You may start slowly and gradually increase the time until you reach at least 30 minutes per day. It will not only energise you but help you to keep your weight in control and above all give you new confidence and raise your self-esteem. Brisk walking is one of the best forms of exercise. It can give you three times the normal amount of oxygen you would otherwise get.

Jogging

Jogging an excellent for heart, lungs and circulation. The  more you jog, the more you burn calories and stronger your muscles become. Almost anyone of any age can jog safely, even if your health is poor, provided your doctor approves of it. You do not have to achieve any particular speed, nor is it necessary to jog every day. Building up stamina you may gradually jog for 15 minutes three times a week, more if you can manage it.

Running

 Running is an excellent all-round exercise for the heart and lungs, muscle strength and endurance. Running is only for the fit and healthy. It is generally unsuitable for anyone over the age of 40 unless they have been running since their younger days or else, they need to prepare for it with another sport or regular

jogging. To build up slowly to the goal set, begin with a mixture of jogging, running and walking to avoid strain on the muscles and heart.

Skipping

Skipping can form a part of the body-building programme, to strengthen the muscles or it can be used to shape figure, by tightening the muscles and loose flesh, making the thighs and calves firmer and shapely and improve posture. Either way, skipping is a good warm-up activity, promotes stamina and coordination and is a good exercise for the heart and lungs. And the best part of it is that it requires a small investment of a skipping rope with your time. Aim to build up to 15 minutes a day.

Cycling

Cycling is an excellent aerobic exercise for the legs, for the heart and for the lungs. Age, arthritis, heart or lung conditions, including asthma, are no bar to cycling, providing you have first consulted your doctor.

Swimming

Swimming is a wonderful and safe way to exercise, as water provides support, so you do not strain any part of your body. This is particularly useful when you are overweight. Thirty minutes of sustained swimming a day increases your stamina, suppleness and strength. It also tones your body and who does not like a well-toned body. Elderly people with arthritis problems are advised to walk in the water. In recent years, water aerobics has become a very popular and enjoyable sport.

Badminton

Badminton is an indoor game, which promotes suppleness throughout the body and builds up powers of endurance. Played vigorously, badminton is a fine exercise for the heart and lungs. As an overhead game, it is especially good for strengthening the back and shoulders and improving posture. Although it is strenuous at a high level, you can enjoy a more social game without over-exertion, particularly mixed doubles. Provided you are reasonably fit, you can take up badminton well into middle age.

Squash

Squash is the fastest game on two legs. Playing for about 30 to 45 minutes will help lose weight, make you more supple, faster on your feet and improve your staying power. Being an indoor game, it can be played throughout the year.

Table tennis

You are interested in a muscular body; this is the game to be played with full-body exertion. However, on a lesser level, the game exercises the lungs and heart, gets you on your toes and improves coordination.

Tennis

A hard game of singles burns up calories, exercises the heart and lungs, increases suppleness and helps in tightening of

stomach muscles in particular and can be still fun. A gentle game of mixed doubles tennis is fun along with the exercising your entire body.

Dancing

All forms of dancing are an excellent exercise and most importantly enjoyable. They aid coordination, flexibility, and suppleness. Dance is good for the heart and lungs and if done energetically, will even help reduce weight. There are several forms of dance to choose from, such as Indian classical dance, folk dance, western dance, ballroom dance, modern dance, and so on.

Callisthenics

Callisthenics is getting weight training benefits by using your own body to build muscles. It includes push-ups, pull-ups, sit-ups, lunges, calf raises and many more. You can do these without any equipment. Weight training and callisthenics are a part of a holistic approach to exercise plus they build strong bones and muscles. Stretching promotes flexibility and can serve as a good warm-up prior to exercise.

Pilates

Pilates is a form of exercise, which has become popular in recent years. It consists of precise movements requiring control and form. It emphasises on proper alignment, centring, concentration, breathing and flowing movements.

Tai Chi

Tai Chi is an ancient Chinese form of meditation expressed through slow, graceful and dance-like movement. It involves and benefits the mind and the body. It involves

slow smooth movements with rhythmic abdominal breathing. It's great for older people, especially those who suffer from arthritis. Tai Chi movements help improve muscle mass, strength, stamina, balance, coordination, flexibility and tones muscles.

Massage

While more research is needed, scientists have found evidence to support the idea that massage therapy can provide mental health benefits., clinical trials suggest that massage therapy may help relieve depression. It may also be a helpful addition to your overall treatment plan.

During massage therapy, a therapist will manipulate your muscles and other soft tissues to enhance their function, promote relaxation, or both.

Massage therapy has been used in China for more than 3,000 years. Some practitioners believe it can help ease feelings of depression. They suggest that touch releases hormones in your body that create a sense of emotional connection. Massage may help calm your mind and improve your mood, as well as ease physical aches and pains.

How can massage therapy help relieve depression?

When your muscles and connective tissues become stiff or rigid, it can cause pain and limit your movement. Massage therapy can help relieve this tension in your muscles and connective tissues. It also increases your blood flow and promotes relaxation.

If you have depression, massage therapy probably won't cure your condition. But it may help relieve the physical symptoms associated with it. For example, massage may help alleviate sluggishness, back pain, joint pain, and muscle aches. It can also help relieve fatigue and sleeping problems.

What does massage therapy involve?

During massage therapy, your therapist will rub, stretch, and apply pressure to muscles in your body. Some styles of massage involve over-the-clothes touching. Others involve direct contact with your skin, often with scented oils. Some involve acupuncture needles, warm stones, or complex twisting poses.

Here are some common types of massages:

Swedish massage:

In this common method, your therapist will apply smooth, circular, kneading actions to your muscles.

Chair massage:

In this method, you will sit on a special chair and lean forward into a headrest. This is a good introduction to massage since the sessions are usually short and don't require you to remove any clothing.

Deep tissue massage:

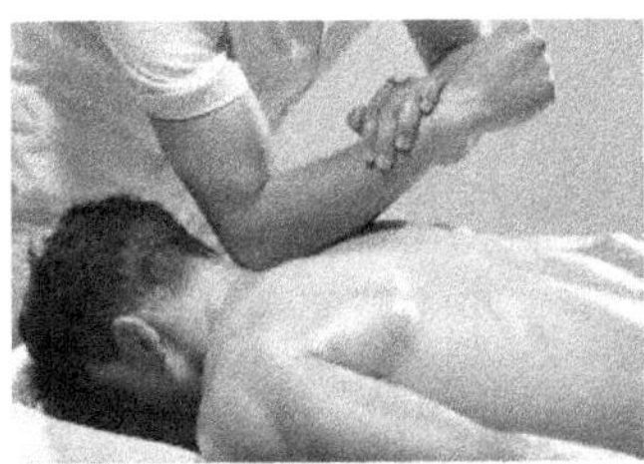

Your massage therapist may use this method to treat tight muscles caused by stress or other problems. They will focus on the muscles closest to your bones, as well as their connective tissues.

Shiatsu:

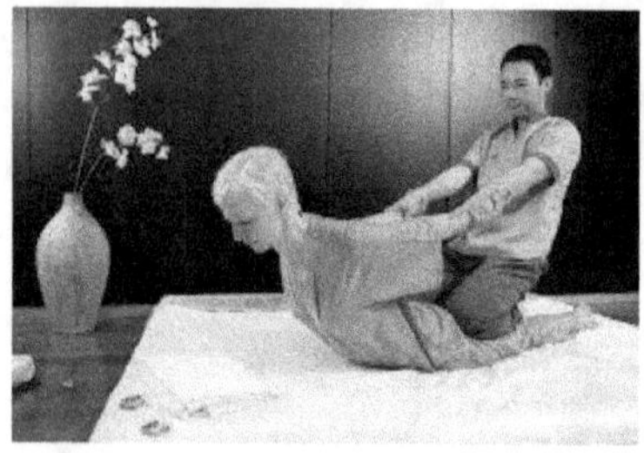

In this technique, your therapist will apply firm pressure to specific points on your body, much like acupuncture. The pressure is firmer than in many types of massage, but it rarely produces stiffness afterwards.

Reflexology:

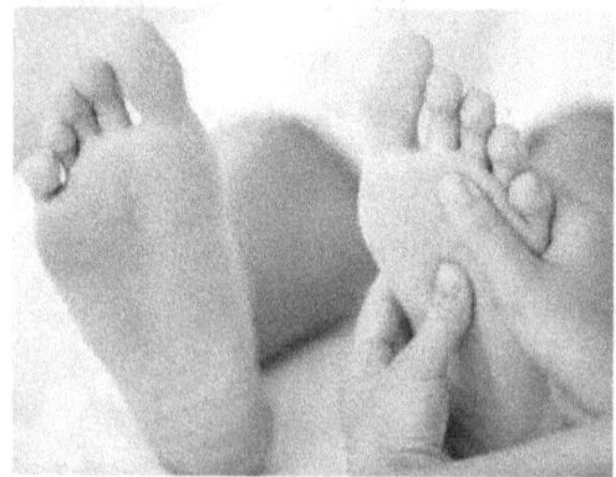

In this type of massage, your therapist will apply pressure to areas of your feet that are believed to correspond with other systems and organs in your body.

Aromatherapy massage:

In this method, your therapist will combine massage with scented oils to help reduce stress or boost your energy.

Hot stone massage:

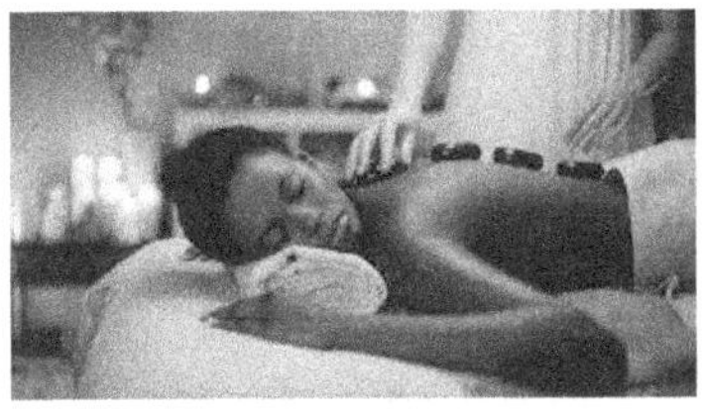

During this method, your therapist will place warm flat stones on your body to help relax your muscles. They will also apply pressure to the stones to relieve muscle tension.

Sleep

Energize yourself with well-earned sleep sleep
"There is only one thing people like that is good for them; a good night's sleep."

-E. W. Howe

No matter how much modern society steers us toward less

sleep, we know that adequate sleep is a vital trusted source to good health, brain function, and emotional well-being.

Most adults need about 7 or 8 hours of sleep every night. If you are feeling drowsy during the day or just generally feel lethargic or tired, you may be your body's way of telling you to sleep more.

Here are a few tips to help you build a better sleep routine:

1. Write down how many hours of sleep you get each night and how rested you feel. After a week, you should have a better idea of how you're doing.
2. As the saying goes "Early to bed and early to rise makes a person healthy, wealthy and wise", hence, go to bed and wake up at the same time every day, including weekends.
3. Reserve the hour before bed as quiet time. Take a bath, read a book, listen to some relaxing music or do something to unwind yourself.
4. Avoid heavy eating and drinking before bedtime.
5. A dark, cool, and quiet bedroom definitely helps.
6. Invest in a good mattress.
7. If you have to take a nap during the day, try to limit it to 20 minutes.

If you consistently have problems sleeping, consult your doctor.

Chapter 7

***

You become what you Eat

If you are passionate about living a full, healthy, happy life, then a balanced, plant-based diet is essential to this. In addition to being mouth-wateringly tasty, vegan cuisine is often nutritious, wholesome, and easy to make yourself.

A plant-based, wholefood diet not only makes you healthy but also helps fight depression.

A plant-based diet does much more than improve your physical health in a short amount of time. It can also be a great way to improve your mood, as well. It's a strange effect, really, considering that the media and food industry promotes foods such as fish, Greek yoghurt, and even poultry or red meat as prominent "mood-boosters" or imperative foods to consume in an ancestral type diet.

Yet, a plant-based diet that full of unadulterated vitamins and minerals straight from the earth, which is where animals get their nutrients from, is the best way to improve your health and mood.

What is veganism

Simply put, veganism is abstinence from the use of animal products in both diet and lifestyle.

"Veganism may be defined as a way of living that seeks to exclude, as far as possible and practical, all forms of exploitation of, and cruelty to, animals for food, clothing, or any other purpose. In dietary terms, it refers to the practice of dispensing with all animal products, including meat, fish, poultry, eggs, animal milk, honey, and their derivatives."

- International Vegetarian Union

Why people adopt vegan lifestyles

People choose veganism for various reasons, including environmental, ethical, and health considerations. Whilst a vegetarian diet avoids meat and fish, a vegan diet excludes animal products altogether.

Some of the ethical reasons people choose to lead a vegan lifestyle include:

- animal welfare issues and the objection to using animals as commodities

- environmental issues directly associated with animal agriculture (such as air pollution and contaminated drainage from factory farming into water supplies) and to help lessen our over consumption of resources including land, water, and fossil fuels
- adopting veganism as a part of the solution to world hunger by more efficiently using our planet's food resources

Plant-based foods that grow in organic soil are the absolute best source of vitamins and trace minerals your brain and body need to feel their best. Calcium, magnesium, zinc, copper, Vitamin A, Vitamin C, amino acids that make up protein, and even omega 3s can all be obtained through plant-based foods.

Here are 10 ways a plant-based diet can affect your mood and the foods that offer the most benefits for each purpose.

1. Magnesium

Magnesium is one of the most overlooked, necessary minerals one needs on any diet, plant-based or not. It's essential for energy, fighting off headaches, improving sleep health, and regulating your mood. Magnesium is also very competitive with calcium, which makes it even more important to consume on a regular basis. Plant-based foods are loaded with high-quality magnesium, while most animal foods have none.

The best sources of magnesium includeall nuts and seeds, cacao, whole grains, coffee, and leafy greens. Bananas, sweet potatoes, and butternut squash also contain decent amounts.

2. Calcium

Calcium is an important nutrient for calming the nerves and keeping our bones healthy. Most plant-based eaters know you don't need to eat dairy to get your fill. Calcium can lower your blood pressure, aid in healthy sleep cycles, treat anxiety, and keep your hair, nails, and teeth in good health.

The best sources of calcium includeleafy greens, seaweed, almonds, broccoli, figs, chia, sesame seeds, some beans, tofu, and non-dairy milk like soy, coconut almondand.

3. Iron

Now, this little fact will really surprise those out there that believe meat is the only source of high-quality iron. Plant-based foods are packed with iron and yes, your body can use this iron just as efficiently as it can meat. For one, plant-based foods come with none of the side effects that meat does, such as saturated fats and acidity. Next, some sources of plant-based iron are actually higher than their animal-based counterparts. Iron is important for your mood because it shuttles oxygen to the brain and provides energy to the body.

Here are the best sources: spirulina, pumpkin seeds (pepitas), cacao, almonds, chia, leafy greens, beans, raisins, mulberries, legumes, and whole grains.

4. Protein

Once again, you don't need meat to get your fill of high-quality nutrients, including protein. The question people ask most often regarding a plant-based diet is "Where do you get your protein?"

But why is protein important for your mood? Well, for starters, amino acids that makeup protein help your neurotransmitters function properly. This can ward off depression, anxiety, and also just make you feel better overall. Protein also keeps you lean and toned, and it gives you strength and stamina.

Plant-based foods that are packed with high-quality protein include spirulina, chia, pumpkin seeds, almonds, quinoa, millet, oats, rye, buckwheat, tofu, soybeans, lentils, beans, and tempeh.

5. Omega 3s

Plant-based foods are also loaded with omega 3 fatty acids, 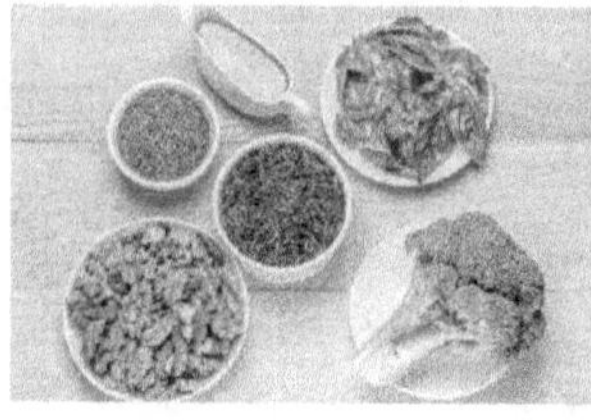 which are vital for healthy brain function, along with heart and skin health. You absolutely do not have to eat fish to get enough omega 3 fatty acids in your diet, especially considering that fish obtain their omega 3 fats directly from algae. Omega 3 fatty acids are anti-inflammatory and help fight off joint pain, along with boost your mood and give you a more positive outlook.

The best sources of omega 3s from plant-based foods include spirulina, chia seeds, hemp seeds, flax seeds, pumpkin seeds, walnuts, and even leafy greens.

6. Non-Acidic

 Plant-based foods are overall very alkaline. Even the most acidic plant-based foods don't compare to the acidity of fish, dairy, meat, and poultry. Plant-based foods also contain a wealth of vitamins and minerals, which help contribute to their overall nutritional benefits. The more acidic your body, the less vitality you'll have overall. You may notice joint pain, stomach problems, and an overall lack of zest for life. An acidic body can also lead to ageing, along with other health issues to be aware of.

The most alkaline plant-based foods includeall leafy greens and vegetables, apples, pears, ripe bananas, winter squash, spirulina, wheatgrass, all green powders, hemp seeds, pumpkin seeds, and sunflower seeds. Sprouts and fermented foods are also excellent for aiding in alkalinity. Making green smoothies and juices is an easy way to improve your alkalinity, along with a raw foods diet.

7. Digestion

Plant-based foods are also wonderful for digestion! Even if you have digestive problems when you first eat a plant-based diet, there are some helpful things you can do to turn this around quickly. Overall, a plant-based diet eliminates acidic wastes, saturated fats, and harmful proteins found in animal-based foods. This improves your mood since your digestion is "your second brain" as they say. When your digestive system is struggling, your mood takes a major hit.

Here are the best plant-based foods to improve digestion: leafy greens, sprouted foods, fermented foods such as tempeh and miso, ripe fruits, soaked grains, raw nuts and seeds, coconut meat, and root vegetables. If you tolerate them, beans and legumes are also great sources of fibre but take it slowly and see how they work for you before diving in headfirst.

8.Healthy Fats

Now, let's talk plant-based fats (which are one of my favourite food categories!) While I love my leafy greens and veggies, healthy fats are a very important part of taking care of your mood on any diet – plant-based or not.

When you ditch the harmful animal fats, laden with cholesterol, you're only left with nature's finest plant-fats. Even those that contain saturated fats are completely cholesterol-free and beneficial to the brain. Just be sure to avoid processed and packaged foods that are high in fat, since those are refined and not beneficial to your mood or any other aspect of your health. Healthy fats come with many health benefits, so long as you consume them smart and in proper portions.

Here are some of the best sources of plant-based fats :avocado, all nuts and seeds, coconut, and cacao and dark chocolate (avoid those with milk and refined sugar). Even some grains like oats and quinoa have a little fat, so eating a variety of foods can help you get enough.

9. Carbohydrates

Carbohydrates are essential for producing serotonin, the feel-good hormone in the brain. Carbs are found in all plants and not in animal foods at all. If you're a fan of the low-carb diet, but seem to have a low mood all the time, this is something you may want to consider. Plant-based foods are filled with good carbs that help promote a balanced mood, help regulate your sleep, and even help benefit your weight if you portion them out between meals. Your body and brain need carbs, just from the right sources and not from refined foods.

Here are the best sources of healthy carbs on a plant-based diet:fruit, whole grains (preferably gluten-free), beans, nuts, seeds, greens and root vegetables, legumes, and sprouted grains. Leafy greens also contain carbs but not as much as these other foods. Be sure you get a variety of plant-based foods in your diet and you'll be well on your way to getting all the carbs you need for a well-balanced mood.

10. Variety

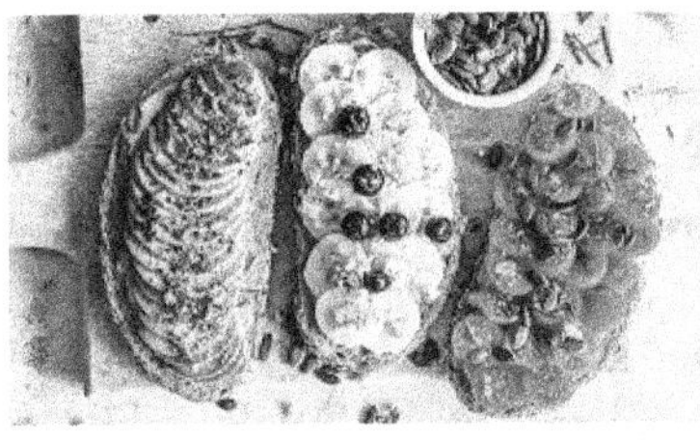

Lastly, one of the best things about a plant-based diet for your mood is the variety of foods you have to choose from. Plants far outweigh animal foods when it comes to choices. You can only do so many things (especially healthier options) with animal-based foods, but the possibilities are endless when it comes to plant-based foods. Why is this good for your mood? For one, you'll hardly ever miss out on nutrients if you eat a whole-food, plant-based diet and your mood will naturally be enhanced through all the variety of foods you eat. Secondly, plant-based foods have so much variety, you're more likely to be excited about preparing healthy meals, which will, in turn, give you mood benefits.

So many people change their diet to be plant-based for their health. More and more of us are discovering a truly healthy life when we stop eating meat, dairy and poultry products and fill our tummies with whole grains, vegetables, beans and fruit.

Others of us become vegetarian or vegan to create a lighter footprint on the planet. Again, there is not much dispute about the facts: animal food production contributes to the destruction of rain forests; the loss of topsoil; the contamination of waterways and air pollution. A plant-based diet creates a lighter footprint on our fragile planet.

Finally, whether or not you support the work or style of organizations like PETA, there is little argument in favour of factory farming. Most of us are horrified by the filth and cruelty that goes into farming animals commercially for human consumption.

Okay, but can eating a plant-based diet result in a more compassionate people? In my view, yes. But it's not just me. So many ancient traditions of spiritual practice eschew animal flesh, from Buddhism to Catholics not eating meat on Fridays to Taoist teachings. See, sparing life -- in any form -- by and for individual people, as well as for the animal is an act of compassion, whether conscious of it or not. It can be seen as the soul's ultimate merge with divine grace or karma or whatever you choose to call it.

In the end, whether you turn to a balanced, plant-based diet for health or for ethics, you receive the gift of "insurance" that you have reduced your risk of becoming a disease statistic as well as reducing the stress on our over-burdened healthcare system. You also remove your support from industries that are socially and environmentally reprehensible and are destroying our collective health.

To live a bit more lightly and sustainably on the planet is to do something tangible and constructive for both our present health and for future generations. And while it's true that becoming a vegetarian may not lead one to spiritual enlightenment just by what we choose to eat, we live in a time when there is a growing awareness of the interconnectedness of all life. Choosing compassion -- in any form -- can help to strengthen our connection with the spirit of life around us.

Chapter 8

****

Break Free

All said and done the million-dollar question to be asked to oneself remains, which is, "Do I really want to be happy?" You might think this to be an absurd question. You might say "Why would I even read a self-help book on happiness if I did not want to be happy."

Wait! Before you get annoyed at me, take a moment close your eyes, and be still. Think to yourself "Do I have some advantages in being miserable?". Think about all aspects of your life. Family, friends, social, religious, career, etc.

Charles Dickens wrote about a prisoner who was locked up for many years in a dungeon. After serving his sentence, he got his freedom. He was brought out from his cell into the bright daylight of the open world. This man looked all around and after a few moments, was so uncomfortable with his newly acquired freedom, that he asked to be taken back to the confines of his cell. To him, the jail, the fetters, and the darkness were more familiar, secure, and, comfortable than accepting the change of freedom and an open world.

Human nature generally resists change. Change is uncomfortable. Regardless of its positive or negative effect, change can often be stressful. Sometimes we get so comfortable with our negativity that even when the change is for the better, we don't want to accept it.

I love this story from the Bible. A man lay helplessly by the pool of Bethesda. This wasn't just any pool. It was rumoured that angels came periodically and stirred the water, and whoever dived in first received miraculous healing. Needless to say, people flocked from near and far for a chance to participate in the phenomenon.

However, this one man, sick for thirty-eight years, could never make it to the pool fast enough. It was a bit of a hopeless situation for him.

One day Jesus sees him lying there and knows that he has already been there for a long time. He says to him, "Do you want to be healed?"

You might think this to be a ridiculous question because obviously, he wants to be healed.

Or, does he really?

It's fascinating that when the sick man answered Jesus, he didn't give a simple yes or no. He offered an excuse. "Sir, I have no one to put me into the pool when the water is stirred up, and while I am going someone steps down before me."

Think about it. This man has been sick for thirty-eight years. He's comfortable in his disease by this point. He's resigned himself to being the victim and blaming others. He's having a pity-pool-party.

"Do you want to be healed?". "Do you want to be happy"

Resignation is a dangerous thing.

Jesus gave this man back a sense of purpose. He freed him from the bonds of self-pity, pride, fear, discouragement, hopelessness, and resignation, all in one amazingly-effective command.

"Get up, take up your bed, and walk."

What? How? He hadn't even gone into the water yet.

Jesus had invited the man into his own healing process.

Now think about your misery as a sickness. Your emotional wound. Your scar. Your grudge. Your bitterness. Your unforgiveness. That disease that you've formed around you like a wall, effectively keeping out any additional pain and suffering.

You've got used to it. It's like a security blanket. It's scratchy, dirty and damp, but it's your protection now. You talk about getting rid of this blanket, how it's awful, and stinks, and you're so desperate to be free of it. But when anyone tries to tug it away, you hold on tight.

Do you really want to be happy?

Notice how the sick man had resigned himself to lingering near the healing, but not participating in it. How often do we do that? We read self- help books, take coaching, counselling, and therapy. We learn everything there is to learn about happiness. We know the drawbacks of staying unhappy and the benefits of becoming happy.

Maybe that's why Jesus asked him "Do you want to be healed?" He already knew the answer.

But the sick man needed to know the answer.

He needed to participate in his own healing. He needed to face the fact that sometimes, healing can be dangerous. It can even hurt worse than the original wound. Broken bones have to be set. And that setting can first mean re-breaking.

But it's the difference between living your life pool-side, and swimming freely in the abundant sea of happiness. This is the choice you will need to make.

This is not a prescriptive or a directive book. I am not a psychologist. This book is based on my own meandering experiences and tried and tested methods gathered from fellow seekers or masters. What worked for me may not work for you. I do not take credit for any of the methods suggested here. I am just a compiler of methods that I have experienced, practised, and suggested.

Read the book and try out for yourself the remedies given. Discard the ones which do not resonate with you. Continue practising the ones which work for you. In time you might find something else which makes you happy. Or you might find a completely new way of becoming happy. Do it. Don't sit by the poolside. Take a plunge into the rejuvenating lake. Take ownership of your own mental wellbeing.

Be brave enough to break the mind binders, the self-made fetters those bind you to misery.

And take charge and move forward to discover your true and happy self!

"What we are today comes
from our thoughts of yesterday,
and present thoughts build
our life of tomorrow:
our life is the creation of our own mind"
-The Buddha

About the Author

Could there be an any better moment for this book to come out? I think not. We are rendered with an unprecedented situation.

The capricious virus bodes ill for those who aren't attuned to their wellbeing. And being so, our surest bet in the fight against this pandemic with unmitigated transmogrification is our robust health- both mental and physical. Hence, the subject was chosen for this book.

We all know that this too shall pass and, in its passing, the humanity shall be left with an irreversible alteration made to their daily lives which, if employed to our advantage may work wonder for us.

The book that you are holding in your hands shall prove to be instrumental in this quest for maintaining or regaining your well-being.

I have known Sreeti for quite a few years now. It's not that her life is perfect. On the contrary, just like everybody else's, she has her share of joys and sorrows. What sets her apart is that she always exudes happiness. Her happiness is contagious. That's why I feel she is the best person to write on the subject of happiness. I'm sure that this contagion of happiness will be passed on to you by the time you are done reading this book.

Sreeti Amonkar has got a diploma in Theatre Arts and a Master's Degree in Business Management. She has been blogging on personal transformation related topics for quite some time.

She has a decade of experience in acting on television and radio. She has over 20 years of enriching work experience in Training across various industries which include BPO, IT, Manufacturing, Hospitality, BFSI, and Educational sector where Trained individuals from Associate to General Manager levels on behavioral and leadership programs.

As a practitioner of Buddhist philosophy, she believes that the world that we live in, is interdependent, co-existential and symbiotic; and being so, our happiness is only a derivative of this microcosm and everything that it encompasses.

She has, thus, always been a proponent of an ethical lifestyle, be it in going vegan or rescuing animals. She says, that a selfless living exhibited through such acts of kindness can act as a trajectory for one's happiness. She is an accomplished life coach and is well known for bringing positive transformations in her clients' lives.

I'm in awe of the sheer thoughtfulness with which this book has been written and I consider it my privilege to write an introduction to this wonderful woman, who has never stopped inspiring me. I sincerely hope that you will find this book as useful as it has been for me.

Sreeti Amonkar has got a diploma in Theatre Arts and a Master's Degree in Business Management. She has been blogging on personal transformation related topics for quite some time.

She has a decade of experience in acting on television and radio. She has over 20 years of enriching work experience in Training across various industries which include BPO, IT, Manufacturing, Hospitality, BFSI, and Educational sector where Trained individuals from Associate to General Manager levels on behavioral and leadership programs.

As a practitioner of Buddhist philosophy, she believes that the world that we live in, is interdependent, co-existential and symbiotic; and being so, our happiness is only a derivative of this microcosm and everything that it encompasses.

She has, thus, always been a proponent of an ethical lifestyle, be it in going vegan or rescuing animals. She says, that a selfless living exhibited through such acts of kindness can act as a trajectory for one's happiness. She is an accomplished life coach and is well known for bringing positive transformations in her clients' lives.

-Prashant Krushna Prakash Sonawane
Pune, Maharashtra
Dakini Day
17th May, 2020

Professional Certifications of the Author

- Psychodrama Therapy- Indian Institute for psychodrama
- Expressive Arts Therapy- East-West Centre for Counselling and Training
- Certified Life Coach- Arfeen Khan
- Certified L&D Manager- MEHR & CAMI
- Pranic Healing Practitioner
- Certified Master Trainer and Facilitator- MEHR & CAMI
- Certified Instructional Designer- MEHR & CAMI
- Certified Psychometric Test Professional- MEHR & CAMI
- Licentiate T&D Specialist -WHRB-US
- Certified Soft Skills Trainer- Grey Cells HRD
- Certified V&A Trainer – Wipro, Powai
- Certified Behavioural Trainer- Centum Learning, Delhi
- NLP Practitioner – National Federation of Neuro-linguistic Psychology, Florida, USA.
- Diploma in NLP -Shinota Consulting, Bangalore
- 101 – An Introductory Course in Transactional Analysis - ICTA, Cochin
- Emotional Freedom Technique- AAMET, Ahmadabad
- Master of Hypnosis -Maunangini, Vadodara
- Emotional Intelligence-IITD
- Certificate in Mind Power Training- Janshikshan Sansthan, Govt. of India, Vadodara
- Transformation (stress relief through self-hypnosis) – Samatvam, Vadodara
- Master's in Business Administration- HR-GOUN
- Diploma in Dramatics - Kala Academy, Panaji, Goa